FREDERICK DOUGLASS

FREDERICK DOUGLASS

Other titles in the
People Who Made History series:

FREDERICK DOUGLASS

John R. McKivigan, *Book Editor*

Daniel Leone, *President*
Bonnie Szumski, *Publisher*
Scott Barbour, *Managing Editor*
David M. Haugen, *Series Editor*

GREENHAVEN
PRESS ®

THOMSON
———— ✦ ————™
GALE

San Diego • Detroit • New York • San Francisco • Cleveland
New Haven, Conn. • Waterville, Maine • London • Munich

LIBRARY OF CONGRESS CATALOGING-IN-PUBLICATION DATA

Frederick Douglass / John R. McKivigan, book editor.
    p. cm. — (People who made history)
Includes bibliographical references and index.
ISBN 0-7377-1522-7 (lib. : alk. paper) — ISBN 0-7377-1523-5 (pbk. : alk. paper)
    1. Douglass, Frederick, 1818–1895. 2. Douglass, Frederick, 1818–1895—
Influence. 3. African American abolitionists—Biography. 4. Abolitionists—United
States—Biography. 5. Slaves—United States—Biography. 6. Antislavery
movements—United States—History—19th century. I. McKivigan, John R.,
1949– . II. Series.
E449.D75F736 2004
973.8'092—dc21   2002045488

Printed in the United States of America

CONTENTS

waged for a high moral purpose that should not be sacrificed in the name of national reconciliation.

labor for reform. Up to his death, he campaigned for such reforms as temperance, woman suffrage, and black civil rights. Most importantly, he consciously strove to be a role model for younger blacks for personal self-improvement as well as racial advancement.

FOREWORD

In the vast and colorful pageant of human history, a handful of individuals stand out. They are the men and women who have come variously to be called "great," "leading," "brilliant," "pivotal," or "infamous" because they and their deeds forever changed their own society or the world as a whole. Some were political or military leaders—kings, queens, presidents, generals, and the like—whose policies, conquests, or innovations reshaped the maps and futures of countries and entire continents. Among those falling into this category were the formidable Roman statesman/general Julius Caesar, who extended Rome's power into Gaul (what is now France); Caesar's lover and ally, the notorious Egyptian queen Cleopatra, who challenged the strongest male rulers of her day; and England's stalwart Queen Elizabeth I, whose defeat of the mighty Spanish Armada saved England from subjugation.

Some of history's other movers and shakers were scientists or other thinkers whose ideas and discoveries altered the way people conduct their everyday lives or view themselves and their place in nature. The electric light and other remarkable inventions of Thomas Edison, for example, revolutionized almost every aspect of home-life and the workplace; and the theories of naturalist Charles Darwin lit the way for biologists and other scientists in their ongoing efforts to understand the origins of living things, including human beings.

Still other people who made history were religious leaders and social reformers. The struggles of the Arabic prophet Muhammad more than a thousand years ago led to the establishment of one of the world's great religions—Islam; and the efforts and personal sacrifices of an American reverend named Martin Luther King Jr. brought about major improvements in race relations and the justice system in the United States.

Each anthology in the People Who Made History series begins with an introductory essay that provides a general overview of the individual's life, times, and contributions. The group of essays that follow are chosen for their accessibility to a young adult audience and carefully edited in consideration of the reading and comprehension levels of that audience. Some of the essays are by noted historians, professors, and other experts. Others are excerpts from contemporary writings by or about the pivotal individual in question. To aid the reader in choosing the material of immediate interest or need, an annotated table of contents summarizes the article's main themes and insights.

Each volume also contains extensive research tools, including a collection of excerpts from primary source documents pertaining to the individual under discussion. The volumes are rounded out with an extensive bibliography and a comprehensive index.

Plutarch, the renowned first-century Greek biographer and moralist, crystallized the idea behind Greenhaven's People Who Made History when he said, "To be ignorant of the lives of the most celebrated men of past ages is to continue in a state of childhood all our days." Indeed, since it is people who make history, every modern nation, organization, institution, invention, artifact, and idea is the result of the diligent efforts of one or more individuals, living or dead; and it is therefore impossible to understand how the world we live in came to be without examining the contributions of these individuals.

Introduction: Frederick Douglass and the Battle for African American Liberty

Most modern Americans, regardless of race, recognize the name Frederick Douglass as that of the most influential black man of the nineteenth century. This Maryland-born slave rose to become one of the nation's greatest reformers, fighting not only for the freedom of blacks but also for the rights of women. Self-educated, he was a popular orator and a widely read journalist and autobiographer. He advised presidents and held important appointed government offices. Most of all, he was the personification of African American achievement in the face of enormous obstacles.

Douglass was not only the leading representative of nineteenth-century blacks, but he also stood for what was best in American ideals: The document he loved most was the Declaration of Independence. An advocate of morality, economic accumulation, self-help, and equality, he believed in racial pride, agitation against discrimination, and integration of blacks into American society. Often called the father of the modern civil rights movement, Frederick Douglass's achievements predate Booker T. Washington's advocacy of vocational education and economic self-help, W.E.B. Du Bois's calls for protest, and Martin Luther King's nonviolent direct action. Frederick Douglass remains an enduring figure in American history.

Slave Child

Thanks largely to his own autobiographical writings and the dedicated work of his biographers, the details of Frederick Douglass's life are better known than those of any other nineteenth-century African American. He was born on a tobacco plantation on the eastern shore of Maryland with the name Frederick Augustus Washington Bailey. His mother,

Harriet, was a slave, and soon after Frederick's birth, she was hired out to work on another farm. With his mother visiting only infrequently, Douglass was raised by his grandmother. Betsy Bailey was a strong woman, proud of a lineage that she could trace back several generations to a slave "Baly," imported from the West Indies but perhaps born in Africa. In her remote cabin, she raised Frederick until the age of six, when she delivered him to the Wye House plantation, the ancestral base of the powerful Lloyd family. Without advanced warning, Betsy left young Frederick at Wye House and never saw him again as a child, thus ending, according to Douglass biographer Nathan Irvin Huggins, "his only real attachment to family."[1]

Frederick's owner was Aaron Anthony, the Lloyd's principal overseer. Anthony, who some believed was Frederick's father, put the boy to work assisting his cook. Anthony often indulged Frederick and allowed him to serve as a companion of one of the Lloyds' male children. The two roamed the forests and swamps with the young Lloyd shooting game and Frederick retrieving it. Through his contact with the Lloyds, Frederick had a glimpse of an affluent lifestyle far beyond the imaginings of most slaves. As a boy, he sat on the banks of the Chesapeake Bay and dreamed of a better life while watching ships sail by on their way to the corners of the world.

THE EDUCATED SLAVE

A significant turning point in Frederick's life came in 1826, when Anthony "loaned" the young slave to his daughter's brother-in-law, Hugh Auld. Auld was a Baltimore shipwright who wanted Frederick as companion for his own son, Tommy, and as a helper around the house for his wife, Sophia Auld, who had never before had a slave under her control. According to Douglass biographer Dickson J. Preston, "She could no more treat him as an inferior than one of her own children."[2] Sophia Auld even began to teach Douglass to read. When Hugh discovered this he ordered these lessons ended, declaring, as Frederick recalled, "Learning . . . will do him no good, but a great deal of harm, making him disconsolate and unhappy. If you teach him how to read, he'll want to know how to write, and this accomplished, he'll be running away with himself."[3] If anything, Auld's opposition encouraged Frederick to become literate. Frederick bribed local schoolchildren with sweets that he stole from the Auld's kitchen to continue his education until he had mastered reading.

By 1833, Aaron Anthony had died and Frederick became the property of Anthony's son-in-law, Thomas Auld, a storekeeper in the small village of St. Michaels, located on Maryland's eastern shore. After a quarrel between the Auld brothers, Thomas Auld had the fifteen-year-old Frederick returned to him at St. Michaels. Frederick found the routines of village life boring after having lived in Baltimore. He got into serious trouble for attempting to operate a clandestine Sunday school for local blacks. To instill more discipline in this over-indulged slave, Frederick was hired out to work for a year on the farm of the area's most notorious "slave breaker," Edward Covey. Determined to make Frederick a more pliant slave, Covey underfed and overworked the young man. Escalating tensions between the two culminated in a brutal two-hour-long showdown in August 1834 in which Frederick successfully resisted all attempts by Covey to tie and whip him. Historian Waldo E. Martin Jr. judges this fight "the most important event in Frederick's journey from thralldom to liberty. It graphically heralded his lifelong dedication to resistance against oppression."[4]

The following year, Auld hired out Frederick to work on the farm owned by a less strict master, William Freeland. Although Frederick never complained of his treatment by Freeland, he had grown more desirous than ever of obtaining his freedom. He plotted with four other slaves to steal a small boat and sail north to freedom. A fellow slave exposed their conspiracy, probably, and all were arrested and jailed. As the ringleader, Frederick expected to be made an example and "sold south" to the distant cotton fields of Alabama or Mississippi. Instead, Thomas Auld decided to give his slave one last chance and returned him to live with his brother's family in Baltimore. Auld even promised to free Frederick at age twenty-five if he behaved obediently.

THE RUNAWAY SLAVE

Hugh Auld put the teenaged Frederick to work on Baltimore's docks. In time, Frederick acquired the valued skill as a ship caulker, although he had to endure racially motivated attacks from white coworkers. His labor rented out to various shipbuilding companies, Frederick was able to generate considerable revenue for Auld. Perhaps to motivate Frederick to work even harder, Auld allowed the slave to seek out his own employers and to live outside the household. Auld's only requirement was that Frederick weekly turn over the bulk of his wages. He joined a small black Methodist congregation and mixed socially with Baltimore's large free black community. In 1837 or early 1838, he met Anna Murray, a free black originally from the eastern shore who worked as a maid for a wealthy white family. Together, the two planned for a life in freedom. Historians Alan J. Rice and Martin Crawford observe that Douglass's time in Baltimore "had equipped him for a life beyond slavery, providing him with an education and socialization that was a rare privilege for a slave youth."[5]

In September 1838 Frederick escaped from Auld by disguising himself as a free black sailor on shore leave. He boldly took a train to New York City, where Anna ren-

In 1838 Douglass escaped from slavery by disguising himself as a free black sailor on leave.

dezvoused with him and the two were married. For greater security, the couple settled in New Bedford, Massachusetts, where they sought anonymity among the city's large free black population. To make it harder for Auld to discover his new home, he dropped the surname Bailey for Douglass. Although a resident in a free state, Douglass encountered considerable racial discrimination when he sought work. He had to work as a day laborer on the docks rather than a caulker due to the opposition of white artisans. He later recalled, "It was new, dirty, and hard work for me; but I went at it with a glad heart and a willing hand. I was now my own master. It was a happy moment, the rapture of which can be understood only by those who have been slaves."[6] Douglass and his wife also derived great pleasure from joining the city's African Methodist Episcopal Zion Church. Douglass became a lay preacher, and the experience that he gained as a public speaker in the church would prove invaluable in his later career.

By the time Douglass had reached the North in the later 1830s, a small but vocal campaign was under way to try to end or abolish slavery. These abolitionists came from diverse backgrounds. Free blacks played a large role in starting the movement. In the early 1830s, many religiously motivated whites also began to speak out against the physical and moral mistreatment of the slaves. In 1840 the abolitionist movement splintered into a number of competing factions over issues of the most effective tactics to pursue. Some favored working through churches as well as governmental institutions to abolish slavery. In New England, in particular, many abolitionists followed the leadership of the white reform journalist William Lloyd Garrison. These Garrisonians favored a coalition of abolitionists with other reformers pursuing such goals as women's rights, temperance, and pacifism. Douglass attended some abolitionist meetings in New Bedford and heard Garrison lecture. Impressed by the abolitionist's commitment to black rights, Douglass attended a regional abolitionist convention on the island of Nantucket in August 1841. Inspired to speak, Douglass briefly told the audience some of his own experiences as a slave. His novice performance convinced the Garrisonians to recruit Douglass to become one of their traveling lecturers. Initially he only described his personal experiences to curious Northern audiences, always remaining careful not to disclose details that would reveal his true identity. In short time, however, Douglass mastered the abolitionists' full arsenal of arguments against slavery in his speeches. His orations became so erudite that critics of the abolitionists charged that Douglass could never have been born a slave as he claimed. To defend his credibility, Douglass in 1845 published the first of three autobiographies, the *Narrative of the Life of Frederick Douglass*, which provided all of the specific details of his birth, ownership, and life in Maryland.

ABOLITIONIST HERO

His identity as a fugitive slave now public, Douglass's friends warned him that his recapture and return to slavery was a real possibility. For his personal safety, Douglass fled to Great Britain. For nearly two years he toured the British Isles lecturing on behalf of the abolitionist cause. He traveled through Ireland and observed the famine. Also witnessing there the evils of heavy drinking, Douglass was converted to the cause of temperance. In Scotland, he created considerable controversy by his vehement attacks on clergy there who had solicited contributions from American slaveholders. Douglass's enthusiastic reception in Great Britain greatly elevated his self-confidence. In late 1846 English abolitionist sympathizers purchased his freedom from Auld and gave Douglass funds to return to the United States and to start his own newspaper. Douglass left Britain, according to Rice and Crawford, "the finished independent man, cut from a whole cloth and able to make his own decisions about the strategies and ideologies of the abolitionist movement."[7]

The founding of the *North Star* (later *Frederick Douglass' Paper*) in Rochester, New York, in late 1847 marked the beginning of Douglass's development of a personal political ideology. Originally a follower of William Lloyd Garrison, Douglass espoused the Garrisonian tenets that the Constitution was a proslavery document, and that voting lent moral sanction to slavery. He condemned not only the two major political parties of the era, the Whigs and the Democrats, but also the small Liberty Party, founded by abolitionist opponents of Garrison in 1840. Although Douglass's writings at this time strictly followed the Garrisonian line, he detected signs that many white Garrisonians disapproved of his more elevated and independent role in the movement as a newspaper editor. Offended by what he viewed as paternalism, Douglass's loyalties began to waiver. In his editorial columns, he questioned Garrisonian orthodoxy regarding the Constitution and wondered in print whether political means might be effective against slavery.

Located in upstate New York far from the Garrisonian center of strength in New England, Douglass sought out new friends and allies. In 1848 Douglass attended the national convention in Buffalo, New York, that founded the Free Soil Party. Although disappointed that the new party failed to call for immediate emancipation of the slaves, Douglass gave a qualified endorsement to its platform opposing the extension of slavery into western territories. In the early 1850s Douglass came into closer contact with abolitionists in his new home region who supported political abolitionist tactics. Their leader, wealthy landowner Gerrit Smith, impressed Douglass by his absence of racial condescension. In 1851 Douglass merged his financially struggling new paper with a Liberty Party periodical underwritten by Smith. The move marked Douglass's defection from the Garrisonian to the political antislavery camp. Throughout the 1850s, Douglass wavered between support for the anti-extensionist Free Soil Party and its Republican successor and Smith's tiny political abolitionist faction that claimed that the federal government had the constitutional power to abolish slavery.

Douglass's preference for political activism led to his acrimonious expulsion from Garrisonian abolitionists ranks. There were charges that he had been "bought" by Smith's generous contributions. There were even nastier imputations that Douglass's personal life was out of order. Rumors circulated that Douglass had developed an improper intimacy with his white editorial assistant, Julia Griffiths, who had come from England to help him with the *North Star.* Douglass came to believe that the Garrisonians' anger toward him was largely motivated by their paternalist belief that the former fugitive slave should forever remain indebted to his original white sponsors.

Facing difficult financial times with a growing family and the loss of many of his original Garrisonian subscribers, Douglass and Griffiths struggled to keep their antislavery newspaper afloat. Douglass traveled widely lecturing and collecting new subscriptions. Griffiths edited a series of gift books entitled the *Liberty Bell,* the proceeds from which went to Douglass's newspaper. For the 1853 issue of the *Lib-*

erty Bell, Douglass wrote a novella, "The Heroic Slave," one of the earliest fictional works by an African American author. This work was a fictionalized defense of an actual shipboard slave uprising led by Madison Washington in 1841. In 1855 Douglass also published his second autobiography, *My Bondage and My Freedom.* The latter work carried on the *Narrative's* assault on the mistreatment of Southern slaves but also added a lengthy indictment of Northern racial discrimination that Douglass had endured since fleeing Maryland. Douglass biographer William S. McFeely observed that readers of this second autobiography "will find a Frederick Douglas of a far more critical and analytical mind than the one in the *Narrative.*"[8]

FIGHTING FOR FREEDOM

In the 1850s Douglass expanded his leadership in the Northern free black community. He attended major conventions of free blacks and strongly advocated both self-help and civil rights. Douglass often resisted segregation policies on ships and railroad cars at the risk of physical injury. He helped lead campaigns to win equal voting rights for black men in New York. Douglass also publicly battled with such other blacks as Martin Delany and Henry H. Garnet, who advocated emigration to Africa as the best course for the elevation of their race. Douglass also befriended Harriet Beecher Stowe after she published *Uncle Tom's Cabin.* He influenced her to abandon her endorsement of the colonization schemes and to offer financial support to establish a black manual arts college, which never materialized despite Douglass's efforts. Also during these years, Douglass was an active conductor on the famous Underground Railroad. He hid runaway slaves in his own house until he was able to assist them to reach Canada, where they would be safe from recapture by their masters.

In the 1850s Douglass also was drawn deeply into the conspiracy led by white abolitionist John Brown. Douglass met Brown while on an abolitionist lecture tour of Massachusetts and was impressed by the latter's freedom from racial prejudices. Brown was searching for more aggressive means of freeing slaves and devised a plot to lead an armed band into the South via the Appalachian Mountains. Hiding in camps deep in those mountains, Brown's followers planned to raid plantations, free slaves, and eventually foment a massive rebellion. In the mid-1850s Brown and several of his sons migrated to the Kansas Territory and played a well-publicized role in the guerrilla skirmishing there between supporters of creating a free state there and those wanting a slave state. In January 1858 Brown visited Rochester and stayed several weeks as a guest in Douglass's home. There, Brown sharpened his original plan to invade the South and attempted to recruit Douglass into the conspiracy. With a family of five children to support, Douglass rejected these entreaties but helped Brown find supporters in both black and white abolitionist circles. As historian David W. Blight observed, Douglass "did not lack physical courage, he was simply too much a realist to join the Harpers Ferry raid. Douglass was also wise enough to know that rhetoric was his best weapon."[9] After Brown's attack failed, authorities uncovered documents linking Douglass to the plot. Fearing arrest, Douglass fled first to Canada and then to Great Britain. Only after the furor died down the following year did Douglass believe it safe to return to Rochester. For the remainder of his life, Douglass strongly championed the memory of John Brown as a martyr for freedom.

Shortly after Douglass's return from abroad, the nation's attention turned to the crisis produced by the election of Republican Party candidate Abraham Lincoln to the presidency. Douglass reluctantly endorsed Lincoln, although he criticized the weakness of the Republican platform that opposed only the spread of slavery to the western territories. Eleven slaveholding states, however, believed that President Lincoln posed a dire threat to the institution of slavery and seceded. Soon the nation was plunged into a bloody civil war. Initially Douglass, in his editorial columns, was critical of Lincoln for failing to make abolition the North's war goal. Following the president's issuance of the Emancipation Proclamation in 1863, Douglass became an energetic supporter of Lincoln and the Union cause. According to Blight, Douglass's "millennialist interpretation of the war caused him to see the conflict as a cleansing tragedy, wherein the nation had been redeemed of its evil by lasting grace."[10] He crisscrossed the North laboring as a recruiter of black soldiers. Two of his three sons joined the famous Fifty-fourth Massachusetts Infantry Regiment and served with distinction. Douglass personally met three times with President Lincoln in Washington and advised him on the best ways to

THE UNITED STATES AT THE BEGINNING OF THE CIVIL WAR

Free States
Slave States
Free Areas That Later Allowed Slavery

employ blacks in the military effort. In later years, Douglass appreciatively recalled that Lincoln had received him graciously at the White House and listened to his recommendations respectfully.

RECONSTRUCTION

When the Civil War ended in 1865, so, too, did the life of the reform-minded president. An assassin's bullet cut short Abraham Lincoln's potential and severed Douglass's tie to the White House. Still, the friendly treatment by Lincoln, coupled with the Republicans' support for the Thirteenth Amendment ending slavery, made Douglass a staunch Republican for the remainder of his life. As a powerful orator with a large following among both African Americans and white abolitionists, Douglass was recruited by the Republicans to stump in both presidential and state election campaigns. A loyal party worker, and an acknowledged leading black Republican, Douglass received a number of political appointments during the postbellum years, including the offices of U.S. marshal (1877–1881) and recorder of deeds (1881–1886) for the District of Columbia and minister resident to the Republic of Haiti (1889–1891). Booker T. Washington noted that Douglass regarded these government appointments "to mean some fresh recognition of the worth of the Negro race."[11]

Another major reason for Douglass's strong partisan loyalties was the condition of his fellow blacks in the former
slave states. During the period immediately following the
Civil War, dubbed Reconstruction, Republicans attempted to
assist freed slaves to attain full citizenship and economic opportunities. Many Southern whites resisted such efforts politically through the Democratic Party and violently through
groups such as the Ku Klux Klan. As Democrats gradually
regained control of Southern state governments, Douglass
advised blacks to remain loyal to the party of Lincoln because "the Republican party is the ship and all else the sea."[12]

Inside the Republican Party, Douglass aligned with the
stalwart faction, believing that white politicians such as
Ulysses S. Grant, John A. Logan, and Roscoe Conkling had a
stronger record of support for civil rights than competing Republican leaders. Douglass particularly was displeased with
the relative indifference that Rutherford B. Hayes, James A.
Garfield, and James G. Blaine displayed toward black rights.
Nonetheless, Douglass fought against any suggestion that the
African Americans split their votes between the two major
parties to gain more leverage with each. In speeches directed
toward white audiences, Douglass strongly counseled against
concessions to the growing mood of sectional reconciliation.
He reminded Northerners that "there was a right side and a
wrong side in the late war which no sentiment ought to cause
us to forget."[13]

In 1870 Douglass relocated to Washington, D.C., where he
assisted two sons in editing a weekly political newspaper,
the *New National Era.* He briefly headed the Freedman's
Savings Bank, but he found that institution to be so financially unstable that he closed it. He campaigned on behalf of
his race for passage and ratification of two more constitutional amendments: the Fourteenth, to recognize black citizenship; and the Fifteenth, to confer the vote on black males.
The latter proposal produced a serious quarrel between
black leaders and many proponents of woman suffrage. The
latter favored an amendment to enfranchise all adults, male
and female, black and white. Douglass had steadfastly supported the women's rights campaign since his attendance at
the Seneca Falls Convention in 1848, but he felt that com-
bining that cause with black male suffrage would likely defeat both at that point in time. After the successful ratification of the Fifteenth Amendment, Douglass went back to

work for woman suffrage and campaigned for that cause until his death. He told an 1888 audience that "the government that excludes women from all participation in its creation, administration and perpetuation, maims itself, deprives itself of one-half of all that is wisest and best for its usefulness, success, and perfection."[14]

During the post–Civil War decades, Douglass was a sought-after lecturer. He toured the country to speak on such diverse topics as ethnology, photography, self-made men, and the Protestant Reformation. He also used the podium to advise black audiences about the virtues of education, enterprise, and thrift. In 1879 he became enmeshed in a serious controversy among black leaders when he advised Southern blacks not to migrate to the prairie states but to remain in the South and struggle there for full equality. Black opponents charged that Douglass was losing touch with the grim realities facing most members of his race. Douglass also was the center of a second, more personal controversy when, following the death of his wife, Anna, in 1882, he married a younger white woman, Helen Pitts, who had been his secretary at the recorder of deeds office. Some other black leaders publicly criticized Douglass for marrying outside his race. His own children also had difficulty accepting Helen into the family, but in time their relationship became cordial if not intimate.

DIPLOMAT

Perhaps to escape this uncomfortable climate, Douglass and Helen departed on a lengthy honeymoon tour of Europe and the Near East in September 1886. During these travels, Douglass had enjoyable reunions with many aging colleagues from abolitionist days, including his former editorial assistant, Julia Griffiths, who had returned to live in her native England. The Douglasses eventually moved on to visit many important historical landmarks in France, Italy, and Greece. The highpoint of this tour for Douglass was a stop in Egypt. Douglass got to view Africa firsthand and climbed to the top of the Pyramid of Cheops. This last stop enhanced Douglass's appreciation of the African contributions to classical civilization.

Soon after his return to Washington, Douglass campaigned vigorously for the election of Republican Benjamin Harrison to the presidency. After Harrison won that office, he appointed Douglass to serve as the U.S. minister plenipotentiary to the Caribbean island republic of Haiti. Some black leaders felt that Douglass had been slighted by the offer of this minor diplomatic post, but he regarded the appointment as a serious responsibility to undertake. According to McFeely, Douglass regarded Haiti as the symbol of "the liberation and autonomy of black people" and did not want it "exposed to the contempt of an insensitive white minister."[15]

The history of Haiti throughout the nineteenth century was one of political instability. It was Douglass's job to represent the United States before the government of Florvil Hyppolite, who had come to power after a bloody civil war. The United States had given crucial assistance to Hyppolite in that conflict and now expected him to comply with their request for the long-term lease of a naval coaling station at Mole St. Nicholas in the country's northwest corner. Douglass loyally presented the American request for control of the Mole to the Haitian government. Fearing this to be only the first of many such requests for concessions, Hyppolite stalled in responding. Impatient, the Harrison administration dispatched the Atlantic fleet to Haitian waters, and its admiral assumed direction of the Mole negotiations from Douglass. When Hyppolite continued to resist, Harrison allowed the crisis to be defused by withdrawing the fleet. Douglass took this opportunity to resign his diplomatic post and later voiced his disapproval of all attempts to coerce the Haitians to cede territory against their will. Faced with inalterable Haitian opposition, the Harrison administration eventually gave up its pressure for a naval base lease.

LESSONS OF THE HOUR

Douglass had been back at his Washington home for only a year from his diplomatic mission when he received a request from Hyppolite to serve the Haitian government. In 1892 a mammoth international fair, known as the World's Columbian Exposition, was to be convened in Chicago to commemorate the four hundredth anniversary of Christopher Columbus's first voyage to the New World. The Haitians funded a modest pavilion to display their nation's agricultural and handicraft products. To head that pavilion and speak on Haiti's behalf at the numerous events planned during the year-and-a-half long exposition, President Hyppolite called on Douglass. The appointment demonstrated that the Haitians did not hold Douglass to blame for the bullying their country endured over the Mole St. Nicholas.

Douglass accepted the post and, along with Helen, settled temporarily in Chicago. As anticipated, he made several major orations proclaiming the accomplishments of the Haitians and inferentially of all peoples of African descent. During the exposition, Douglass also joined other blacks in protesting the lack of displays of any African American mechanical and intellectual achievements. Douglass, furthermore, used his time in Chicago to meet numerous young blacks, whom he encouraged to dedicate themselves to the cause of racial uplift.

One important acquaintance Douglass made in Chicago was Ida B. Wells. A young journalist, Wells was struggling to expose the racist motivations of a recent wave of lynchings of Southern black males. Inspired by Wells's fervor, Douglass took up the antilynching cause. In his last years, he traveled widely to deliver his powerful "Lessons of the Hour" address, which vehemently denounced the lynchings. Even more significantly, Douglass rebuked prominent whites for publicly condoning such outrages. He called on the North, and especially the Republican Party, to remember its commitment to the freedmen and to punish this antiblack barbarity. In his final advice to Americans, he declared, "Put away your racial prejudice. Banish the idea that one class must rule over another. Recognize the fact that the rights of the humblest citizen are as worthy of protection as are those of the highest, and. . . your Republic will stand and flourish forever."[16]

THE LEGACY OF FREDERICK DOUGLASS

Active in the face of advancing years, Douglass attended a women's rights rally in Washington, at the invitation of Susan B. Anthony, on February 20, 1895. When he went home that evening, he prepared to attend another meeting at a neighborhood black church. Douglass suddenly collapsed and quickly died of a heart attack. His passing was mourned nationwide. Five state legislatures adopted resolutions of official regret. Senators and a U.S. Supreme Court justice attended a memorial service for Douglass in Washington. He was buried in Rochester and a heroic statue was erected near the site of his old house there.

Across the nation blacks eulogized their departed colleague. The next generation of African American leaders, headed by Booker T. Washington and W.E.B. Du Bois, examined Douglass's long career and held him up as a role model for younger members of his race. Washington saw him as an archetypal black self-made man, embodying the virtues of hard work, perseverance, and self-control necessary for success in America. Du Bois found inspiration in Douglass's unswerving commitment to destroying all obstacles that white oppressors placed before their race. Twentieth-century civil rights leaders called on Douglass's memory to champion such diverse causes as integration and black nationalism and tactics as different as nonviolent protest, militant confrontation, and political agitation. To this day, Frederick Douglass remains a symbol of the need to continue to struggle until all peoples have achieved equal rights and opportunity.

NOTES

1. Nathan Irvin Huggins, *Slave and Citizen: The Life of Frederick Douglass.* Boston: Little, Brown, 1980, p. 4.
2. Dickson J. Preston, *Young Frederick Douglass.* Baltimore: Johns Hopkins University Press, 1980, p. 87.
3. Quoted in Frederick Douglass, *My Bondage and My Freedom.* Urbana: University of Illinois Press, 1987, p. 92.
4. Waldo E. Martin Jr., *The Mind of Frederick Douglass.* Chapel Hill: University of North Carolina Press, 1984, p. 13.
5. Alan J. Rice and Martin Crawford, *Liberating Sojourn: Frederick Douglass and Transatlantic Reform.* Athens: University of Georgia Press, 1999, p. 1.
6. Frederick Douglass, *Narrative of the Life of Frederick Douglass.* New York: Penguin Books, 1984, p. 150.
7. Rice and Crawford, *Liberating Sojourn.* p. 3.
8. William S. McFeely, *Frederick Douglass.* New York: W.W. Norton, 1991, p. 181.
9. David W. Blight, *Frederick Douglass' Civil War: Keeping Faith in Jubilee.* Baton Rouge: Louisiana State University Press, 1989, pp. 95–96.
10. Blight, *Frederick Douglass' Civil War*, p. 235.
11. Booker T. Washington, *Frederick Douglass.* Philadelphia: George W. Jacobs, 1906, p. 292.
12. Quoted in John W. Blassingame et al., eds., *The Frederick Douglass Papers.* Vol. 4. New Haven, CT: Yale University Press, 1979, p. 298.
13. Quoted in Blassingame, *The Frederick Douglass Papers*, vol. 4, p. 491.
14. Quoted in Blassingame, *The Frederick Douglass Papers*, vol. 5, p. 387.
15. McFeely, *Frederick Douglass*, p. 336.
16. Quoted in Blassingame, *The Frederick Douglass Papers*, vol. 5, p. 607.

CHAPTER 1

DOUGLASS'S EARLY LIFE AS A SLAVE

 FREDERICK DOUGLASS

The Bailey Legacy

Dickson J. Preston

Baltimore journalist and amateur historian Dickson
J. Preston wrote several books on the early history of
Maryland's eastern shore. He researched sources on
that region's history, such as plantation documents,
courthouse records, U.S. Census tracts, and correspondence archives. In the following selection from
his book *Young Frederick Douglass: The Maryland
Years*, Preston utilizes those sources to develop the
family tree of Frederick Augustus Washington Bailey,
later known to the world as Frederick Douglass.
Preston traces Douglass's family back five generations to a slave, Baly, born in 1701 and possibly to
Maryland's Native American residents. From this
evidence, Preston concludes that Frederick Douglass
was proud of his heritage and was firmly rooted in
Maryland's rural culture.

In mellow middle age, Frederick Douglass grew nostalgic
about the Eastern Shore of Maryland, scene of his birth and
childhood as a slave.

"I am an Eastern Shoreman, with all that name implies,"
he proclaimed proudly to an 1877 audience. "Eastern Shore
corn and Eastern Shore pork gave me my muscle. I love
Maryland and the Eastern Shore."

Race-proud, tradition-bound Eastern Shore whites who
heard him may have sneered at such presumption by a Negro, but Douglass had every right to make the claim. His ancestral roots went deep into the Eastern Shore's early history. Not only was he born there, but all available evidence
indicates that his black as well as his unknown white ancestors had lived on the Eastern Shore almost from its beginnings as a part of the Maryland colony.

The public record of his black forebears dates from June
1746, thirty years before the American Revolution, when the

Dickson J. Preston, *Young Frederick Douglass: The Maryland Years*. Baltimore: Johns
Hopkins University Press, 1980. Copyright © 1980 by Johns Hopkins University Press.
Reproduced by permission.

name of his great-grandmother, Jenny or Jeney, appeared in an inventory of slaves belonging to one Richard Skinner, a tobacco planter in the Miles River Neck district of the Eastern Shore's Talbot County.

Jenny was a nursing infant, six months old, when the inventory was taken. Only two adult women, Sue and Selah, were listed as Skinner property; clearly, therefore, one of them must have been her mother. And there was only one adult male, a man named Baly. In the absence of other evidence, he can be presumed to have been Jenny's father. All the other blacks named in the inventory were children ranging in age from five months to nine years, undoubtedly the offspring of Sue and Selah. Thus it is almost certain that Richard Skinner's slaves constituted a family or clan grouping—a man, two women, eight children—that had been established for some years in Talbot County.

The progenitor of the family appears to have been Baly, born about 1701, for it was from him that the family surname of Bailey, by which Douglass first was known, eventually was taken. Where Baly was born, or who his parents were, are questions left unanswered in the mists of recorded early Maryland history. He may well have been descended from slaves who had been in Talbot almost from the time of the county's first settlement around 1660. Or he may have been imported, as were many Talbot County blacks of his generation, from Barbados or some other English colony in the West Indies. . . . The fact that he bore a common English name suggests that he had been associated with English-speaking whites from his childhood; Baileys, under various spellings, had been among the first white settlers of Talbot County.

THE ORIGIN OF THE BAILEY FAMILY

Considering that he was a black slave on the rural Eastern Shore, a surprising amount of information can be gleaned from existing records about Baly. He was about forty-five years old in 1746, when he was recorded as living on the Skinner plantation, and was evidently considered an able worker, since he was valued at forty-five pounds, current money of Maryland. He was still there, an eighty-year-old man, in 1781. Strong circumstantial evidence indicates that he had two wives, and numerous children and grandchildren; but because fatherhood was seldom recognized in Maryland slavery, that must remain speculation.

Even the surroundings in which he spent his adult life can be visualized. The Skinner plantation, on what was then known as Bear Point Creek (now Leeds Creek), was not an especially large or wealthy one, as such estates went in colonial Talbot County. The main house, still extant but now incorporated into a larger mansion called Fairview, was a frame structure with two brick chimneys and gable ends. It was forty-one feet long and twenty wide. There was a separate kitchen, almost as large, with an attic and cellar; the tobacco house, roofed with featheredged shingles, was the largest building on the plantation.

The "quarter" in which Baly and the other slaves lived was built of logs and was probably windowless, with bunks along the walls for sleeping. It was twenty-five by sixteen feet, with a large fireplace at one end used for both heating and cooking, and a substantial brick chimney. Here from ten to sixteen blacks were crowded in communal squalor.

Other buildings on the place were a brick meathouse, ten feet square; a milkhouse; a "chaise house" (carriage house); a long, narrow barn and shed; a necessary house; two corn cribs; a workshop; and a stable. About forty of the three hundred or so acres were "low swamp," and most of the tillable land had been denuded of trees, but there was a fine orchard with more than a hundred apple and twenty cherry trees. At the upper end of the plantation, away from the creek, was a smaller dwelling with its own orchard, tobacco barn, and other outbuildings.

In the 1740s, when Richard Skinner was master, he owned, in additon to 11 human chattels, 108 sheep, 25 cows and calves, 5 steers, 2 bulls, and about 60 swine. As a measure of how blacks were regarded in the eighteenth century, it is worth noting that the same inventory account which listed his slaves by name also gave the names of all his horses: Dragon, Lyon, Squirrel, Maloony, Fenia, Bony, and Sorrel. He had one white servant, bound to him for a term of years, who undoubtedly acted as his overseer.

In such a setting, Baly and the large clan that eventually took his name lived with little or no disruption for more than half a century. Their world, though harsh, was a stable and dependable one. They had nothing to fear from changes of ownership; in all that time no Skinner slave was ever sold away from the Eastern Shore, and only one was ever sold outside the family. Slaves in eighteenth-century Maryland were too valuable, both as productive workers and as status symbols, to be sold or given away lightly; instead, they were handed down from generation to generation, like family heirlooms.

Baly's ancestors had been torn from Africa and subjected to the unknown terrors of slavery in a strange environment; his descendants, in Frederick Douglass's generation, would face similar uprooting. But in Baly's time, at least, slave life had a stability that made it bearable. Security was in the land on which one was born, lived, and died, the seasons that served as calendar, the "white folks" to whom one owed loyalty, and the submerged but tenacious allegiance to a black family.

How strong this family loyalty was among the Baly-Baileys can be surmised from one bit of tangible evidence: the persistence with which given names were passed on from mother to daughter, and even from unacknowledged father to son, through successive generations. While some Eastern Shore slaves, in mockery of their natural dignity, were arbitrarily given such ridiculous names by their masters as Caesar, Pompey, Cato, Jupiter, and the like, the naming of many was left to their slave mothers; and often the name of a beloved older person was the only possession a mother could bestow to give her child a sense of belonging to a particular clan group or family.

Beginning with the original Baly, that name appeared in five successive generations under various spellings (Baly, Bealy, Bail, Baley, Baily) until it finally emerged as Bailey, the family surname. Other given names also turned up with a regularity that could scarcely be coincidental. In addition to the Jenny born in 1745, there was a Jenny who was a young girl in 1781, and another Jenny, granddaughter to the first one, who was a sister of Douglass's mother, Harriet. In at least three generations there were boys named Phil or Phill, and indications are that they were probably father, son, and great-grandson. Selah emerged later as Sillah and Priscilla. Harry-Henry, Bett-Betty-Betsy, Isaac, Sarah, and Sue all were used in one generation after another. Even Augustus, Douglass's original second name, came to him from an uncle who had died shortly before the boy Frederick was born.

In part, this clan feeling among blacks can be linked to their ancestral experience in Africa, where the kin group played a key role in the social structure. But in Maryland, at least, it also reflected their long and intimate contact with an aristocratic white society that placed supreme emphasis on "breeding" and pride of family. However it originated, identity with the kin group was important to eighteenth-century Talbot County blacks, and no family unit is more clearly defined over a longer period than the Baly-Bailey clan. Although its existence had no official recognition, its members were well known to one another. Ancestors were remembered and honored, and children were taught to emulate the skills and virtues of beloved parents, grandparents, aunts, and uncles. The Baileys were a strong and, in their own way, prideful family, with deep roots in their Eastern Shore soil and a long tradition of courage and endurance. That makes it less surprising that they produced, out of the sordidness and poverty of slavery, the flowering genius of a Frederick Douglass. . . .

MATERNAL ANCESTRY

A combination of various sources provides a maternal ancestry for Douglass, in large part confirmed by independent evidence, that reaches back five generations into the early history of the Eastern Shore. In genealogical terms, it may be expressed as follows:

First generation: Baly, born ca. 1701, presumed father of Jenny (Jeney, Jinny), born ca. December, 1745. Sue, born ca. 1721, or Selah, mother of Jeney.

Second generation: Jenny (Jeney), born 1745, mother of Bets (Bett, Betsey), born May, 1774.

Third generation: Bets, born 1774, mother of Harriet (Hariet, Harriott), born February 28, 1792.

Fourth generation: Harriet, born 1792, mother of Frederick Augustus, born February, 1818.

Fifth generation: Frederick, born 1818, took the name Frederick Douglass.

Unfortunately for his peace of mind, Douglass never saw either the private or public records of his birth and ancestry. If he had he would have found answers to questions that haunted him all his adult life: who he was, when he was born, whence he came. And he would have had additional support for his argument that black Americans should not be shut out from the national heritage; for his roots, if he had only known it, went as far back into the beginnings of the American experience as did those of almost any Anglo-Saxon white.

For that matter, they may have reached back even further, into American prehistory. A substantial body of evidence suggests that Douglass was part Indian. Strong family tradition supports this view; "Your cousin Tom Bailey . . . told me that your grandmother [Betsey Bailey] was of Indian descent," Lewis Douglass wrote his father while visiting Eastern Shore relatives in 1865.

Certainly Douglass looked Indian, with his broad forehead, heavy cheekbones, and yellow-brown skin. While he never publicly confirmed that he had an Indian ancestor, perhaps because he wasn't sure the family tradition was true, he gave broad hints of it in his speeches and writings. On one occasion he appeared to boast of an Indian background. In a speech at the Carlisle Indian Institute, he told the assembled student body, "I rejoice beyond expression at what I have seen and heard at this Carlisle School for Indians. I have been known as a Negro, but I wish to be known here and now as Indian."

There are other indications. When Frederick was a child, his master, Aaron Anthony, called him his "little Indian boy." As an adult, he wrote, he was often asked "whether I was not part Indian as well as African and Caucasian?" Douglass did not say how he answered the question, but he did record his answer when he was accosted by a stranger on a Hudson River steamer "who took me for one of the noble red men of the far West." When Douglass replied that he was not an Indian chief but a Negro, he said the man turned away in disgust.

Douglass described his mother, who died when he was about seven, as "of dark, glossy complexion"; but his memory of her suggests that she had an Asian rather than black African cast of features. In the 1850s he came across a drawing of the head of an Egyptian pharaoh, Rameses the Great, in a book on anthropology. "The features . . . so resemble those of my mother that I often recur to it with something of the feelings which I suppose others experience when looking upon the likenesses of their own dear departed ones," he wrote. The author, James Cowles Prichard, cited the head of Rameses as a type that "approaches the Hindoo" rather than the European or African.

Whether or not there was an American Indian strain, Douglass's ancestry was solidly based in an American rather than an African tradition. His black forebears had lived in Talbot County for many years, perhaps more than a century, before his birth. They were thoroughly acclimated to their environment, and their black subculture was attuned to the dominant white society of which they were a subservient part. Inevitably, their group attitudes were absorbed by the boy who was born into the Bailey family in 1818, and were reflected in the character of the mature Douglass. In turn, those attitudes reflected the peculiar social and economic patterns of Talbot County and the Eastern Shore during the colonial period.

A Growing Discontent with Slave Life

Benjamin Quarles

Compared to a majority of other early nineteenth-century slaves, young Frederick Douglass was physically well treated while living and working both on Maryland's eastern shore and later in Baltimore. Psychologically, however, the intelligent young slave grew steadily more discontented after he entered his teen years. As historian Benjamin Quarles observes, the occasional privileges he received and the loose control his masters exerted only made Douglass desire his complete freedom. Quarles's 1948 biography of Frederick Douglass was the first of this historian's seven meticulously researched books on the role African Americans played in U.S. history through the Civil War era.

From some month in the year 1817—the circumstances of his birth are not known—until his escape twenty years later, Frederick Douglass was a part of the institution that he was to denounce for a quarter of a century. That he had been held in bondage became the cardinal fact in his life. His slave background was his springboard into public notice; it gave an authenticity to his invective, it furnished his ram's horn with a fathomless arsenal to sound against the Southern "lords of the lash," and, finally, as his great abilities unfolded, it enabled him to stand forth in dramatic condemnation of an institution that would enthrall a man of his capacity.

Douglass' fame rests largely upon his impassioned outbursts of rhetoric by which he gave vent to an uncompromising hostility to the slave system. The sources of this militant abolitionism are varied. . . . What portion of his hatred of slavery may be traced to the experiences of his days in bondage is difficult to determine.

Benjamin Quarles, *Frederick Douglass*. New York: Atheneum, 1968. Copyright © 1948 by Associated Publishers, Inc. Reproduced by permission.

The man himself is the exclusive authority on the early period of his life. The story, shorn of certain dramatic incidents, is soon told. Of typically obscure parentage, Douglass was born in Talbot County on the eastern shore of Maryland. His knowledge of his mother was "very scanty." Her duties as a slave required her presence at a point twelve miles distant from her young son. Douglass saw her only a few times before she died when he was eight or nine. His father remains anonymous.

The absence of parental care was filled in part by a shrewd, warm-hearted grandmother around whose slave cabin the child's world centered. During these years Douglass led the life of a normal youngster—fishing, roaming the fields, and playing with his numerous cousins. When he was seven he was taken some twelve miles from his birthplace to the residence of his master, Captain Aaron Anthony, on the banks of the river Wye. Captain Anthony, a slave-owner in his own right, was also general overseer for Colonel Edward Lloyd, "the greatest and most successful wheat grower and cattle raiser in Maryland," and the fifth Edward of a historic Maryland family, the Lloyds of Wye.

On the Lloyd plantation Douglass ran errands and did other simple chores. Here he witnessed the harsher aspects of slavery, growing familiar with cold and hunger—privations unsoftened by the attitude of "Aunt Katy," an unsympathetic cook, into whose charge he had been placed.

A turning point occurred during the summer of 1825 when the eight-year-old slave was overjoyed at the decision to send him to Baltimore to a distant relative of Captain Anthony. Here for seven years he served Hugh Auld, as a houseboy minding Auld's son, and then as an unskilled laborer in his ship-yard. This Baltimore period was doubly idyllic compared to the years that immediately followed. The change of ownership as a consequence of the death of Captain Anthony placed Douglass in the possession of Thomas Auld, Anthony's son-in-law, who resided at St. Michaels, some forty miles from Baltimore.

An Intractable Spirit

Inevitably Douglass proved refractory in the new environment. The spirit of insubordination was stimulated by the notions of freedom which had entered his head, and by the more rigorous regimen of the plantation system following the freer city life. Early in 1834 Douglass was hired out to Edward Covey, a small farmer and professional slave-breaker who, as Douglass' master expected, would provide the proper conditioning. For six months Douglass was flogged every week. One day, steeled by desperation, the goaded youth soundly thrashed Covey, who thereupon abandoned the whip for the four remaining months of hire.

During the two years that followed this experience, Douglass' master hired him out to a nearby plantation owner whose technique of handling slaves contrasted sharply with Covey's. But Douglass had now reached the stage of aspiration that only freedom could satisfy. A kind master, an abundance of food, a moderate work assignment, the thrill of conducting an undercover Sunday school—these things were not enough. Furthermore, from Talbot County the runaway journey would be a short one.

To reach free soil Douglass conceived a plan to paddle down the Chesapeake to its head and then strike northward on foot. However, one of the half dozen conspirators prematurely disclosed the plan. As originator of the scheme Douglass was put in chains. But his daring brought unexpected results; for his attempted escape he was not sold to the lower South as was customary. His master, not bad at heart, and troubled about slavery, hoped to induce a more tractable spirit in Douglass by sending him back to Baltimore with a promise of freedom when he reached twenty-five.

For the next two years the young slave worked in the shipyards, first as an apprentice, then as an expert calker. At fast, every penny of his earnings belonged to his master, but finally he persuaded Auld to permit him to bargain for his own employment in return for a weekly payment of three dollars.

A quarrel with Auld in the summer of 1838 hastened Douglass' determination to go north. He chose a familiar stratagem to effect his departure. From a sea-faring friend he borrowed (to be returned by mail) a sailor's "protection," a paper enumerating the physical characteristics of its rightful owner who ostensibly was a free American sailor. To avoid scrutiny Douglass waited until the train, running from Baltimore to Philadelphia, was in motion. To carry off the impersonation he relied on the nautical knowledge he had acquired at the ship-yards. The train conductor, deferring to a man in naval service, was satisfied with the "protection" in the absence of the "free papers" which Maryland law required that all free Negroes carry and produce on demand. Fortunately too the conductor did not compare Douglass' features with those described by the "protection." On September 4 Douglass rode into New York City with his heart beating high.

ATTITUDE TOWARD SLAVERY

Douglass defined slavery as "perpetual unpaid toil; no marriage, no husband, no wife, no parent, no child; ignorance, brutality, licentiousness; whips, scourges, chains, auctions, jails and separations; an embodiment of all the woes the imagination can conceive." Obviously, however, the great hatred he came to bear against the slave system was not traceable in full to Douglass' personal experiences. Many bondmen would have been contented with his lot. Slavery in Maryland was more "enlightened" than in the lower South; town slaves were better fed and less likely to feel the whip than their plantation brothers. Nor, after his young boyhood, did Douglass experience the most heart-rending of slave sufferings—the separation from a beloved family member. He never saw his half-brother or his three half-sisters until he was seven. His acquaintance with them extended over less than half a year before he was sent away. The brief, sporadic visits of his mother under cover of night, and his ignorance of his paternity left in Douglass an absence of sentimental ties whose severance might have resulted in a long-remembered emotional upset.

Douglass' attitude toward his slave status was perhaps grounded less in external circumstance than in psychological make-up. Here was a youth, sensitive, intelligent and ambitious. The slave whippings and deprivations, although neither uncommon nor unusual to a hereditary bondman, left a lasting impression on his plastic mind. The memory of a slave being flogged would make his nights sleepless. He was profoundly moved by the piteous cries and heavy footsteps of the chained gangs in Baltimore, on their way from the slave pen to the general depot. Few human beings, he concluded early in life, could be trusted to exercise absolute power over their fellows with moderation.

He meditated on the coarseness and meagreness of the slave diet as contrasted with the groaning table at the "big house." He meditated on the raiment of his master and his mistress as contrasted with the semi-nudity of the slave

BORDER STATE SLAVERY

Columbia University professor of history Barbara Jeanne Fields is an expert on the treatment of slaves in the upper states of the South during the decades immediately before the Civil War. Fields notes that Frederick Douglass struggled in his autobiographies to explain to readers the less visible ways that slaves suffered in a region where conditions were generally believed to be mild.

In explaining why his boyhood experience departed from the generally accepted picture of slavery in Maryland, Douglass laid particular emphasis upon the isolation of the corner of Talbot County where he lived as a boy. On Edward Lloyd's home plantation, Douglass maintained, slavery could develop its unsavory potential "wrapt in its own congenial, midnight darkness," beyond the restraint of public opinion. Perhaps slavery was mild, he implied, in less self-enclosed parts of the state, where it lay exposed to the "ray of healthy public sentiment." Douglass may have made this concession as a tactical maneuver, in order to retain the confidence of an audience with whose presuppositions he was well acquainted. For the safest generalization seems to be that, in matters concerning the material care and treatment of their slaves, slaveholders in the border states exhibited the same range as their fellows in the lower South. On the other hand, certain routine features of slave life in Maryland, arising from Maryland's special circumstances and taken for granted by public opinion, gave slavery there a flavor for which *benign* and *mild* are hardly suitable terms. During the antebellum years black people in Maryland—slave and free—experienced the agony of slavery's slow death, but not the deliverance. The middle ground imparted an extra measure of bitterness to enslavement, set close boundaries on the liberty of the ostensibly free, and played havoc with bonds of love, friendship, and family among slaves and between them and free black people.

Barbara Jeanne Fields, *Slavery and Freedom on the Middle Ground: Maryland in the Nineteenth Century.* New Haven, CT: Yale University Press, 1985.

whose yearly wardrobe of two shirts and two pairs of trousers was scarcely equal to the vagaries of the thermometer. . . . He held back from the singing and dancing and year-end celebrations. Such festivities he regarded as escapist. To him the slave sang because he was relieved by song "as an aching heart is relieved by tears." Others might spend themselves in emotional outbursts; he would earn his bitter bread in moody silence. Others might don cap and bells to cloak themselves against spiritual bruise; he would see it through unsupported by any avoidance-of-pain mechanism.

Combined with his sensitiveness was an alert intelligence. An aptitude for reflection led him to conduct imaginary conversations. No satisfactory answers were forthcoming to the questions he was always asking himself: "Why am I a slave? Why are some people slaves, and others masters? Was there ever a time when this was not so? How did the relation commence?" In response to his importunities, his religiously-minded Baltimore mistress taught him to read in order that he might come to know the Bible. When his master arrested this instruction, on the ground that "learning" would spoil a slave, the enterprising youth learned how to spell by various ingenious methods. The first pennies he could call his own went for a popular book of declamation, the *Columbian Orator.*

Douglass's Ambition

Douglass was ambitious. He had no capacity for finding happiness in a humble sphere under adverse circumstances. Slavery had always been an enemy to his self-expression. It thwarted him at every turn. If he attempted to gain knowledge, slavery grew suspicious; if he attempted to teach his fellows, slavery cracked the whip; if he attempted to run away, slavery dragged him back to his chains.

The Baltimore environment, with its weak master-slave relationship, gave a stimulus to Douglass' ambition for complete freedom. As a boy on the streets he measured his mind with the minds of his white playmates; as a young man he learned the lessons of self-control and self-discipline. Free and equal in his own mind, he, nevertheless, had little control over his wages and less over his locomotion. About him lived a large free Negro population, possessing, in 1835, ten churches and more than thirty-five benevolent societies. From membership in the latter Douglass, as a slave, found himself excluded. The East Baltimore Improvement Society alone—as a special concession—permitted him to become a member. Through this society he met Anna Murray, and fuel was added to his burning desire to change his status. Escape and freedom would enable him to marry as a man!

The very privileges he had enjoyed made him freedom-conscious. Give a man a bad master, he wrote, and he as-

pired to a good master; give him a good master and he as-
pired to be his own master. By 1838 Douglass was psychologically ready to become his own master. His subsequent
fulminations against slavery were not, therefore, based exclusively on the experiences he underwent, nor, as he
pointed out, did he use the public platform to dramatize his
personal grievance. Rather, he preferred to base his opposition to slavery on the sufferings and hardships of three million slaves whose rights were violated. Yet his own memories must inevitably have entered in. Who, tracing backward
the savor of his personality, can say with certainty:

> This portion of the river of my mind
> Came from yon fountain?

Douglass's Discovery of Oratory

Gregory P. Lampe

The greatest formative incident in young Frederick Douglass's slave life was when the white woman supervising him in Baltimore taught her charge the rudiments of reading. Douglass soon was surreptitiously buying books and beginning a lifelong course of self-education. Years later, Douglass recalled that the most influential reading from his youth was Caleb Bingham's *Columbian Orator*, a popular primer of the era. This volume taught Douglass the techniques of effective public speaking and persuasive argument; skills he would later put to use in his abolitionist career. The following excerpt by Gregory P. Lampe, associate vice chancellor for academic affairs at the University of Wisconsin–Rock County, analyzes the impact of the *Columbian Orator* on the young Douglass. It was the combination of natural abilities and the lessons from Bingham's book, Lampe concludes, that made Douglass into arguably the greatest of all orators in the rhetorical battle over slavery.

In 1826 [Douglass's original master] Aaron Anthony sent Douglass to Baltimore to work for Hugh Auld. Auld had asked his brother-in-law for a young black slave to serve as a companion to his two-year-old son, Tommy. Douglass left the plantation with "inexpressible joy" and with the hope for a better life in Baltimore.

When Douglass arrived in Baltimore, he found a noisy, bustling city—a city experiencing dramatic growth from a small port to a much larger industrial and commercial center linked to international markets. Douglass would soon discover that Baltimore had a sizable free black population, with

Gregory P. Lampe, *Frederick Douglass: Freedom's Voice, 1818–1845.* Lansing: Michigan State University Press, 1995. Copyright © 1995 by Gregory P. Lampe. Reproduced by permission.

687 free black households making up 15 percent of the total households in the city. Altogether, there were 20,000 free blacks living in Baltimore in the 1830s, and they outnumbered slaves by a ratio of five to one. Through churches, schools, and voluntary associations, these free black Baltimoreans fostered an independent community within the larger city. While living in Baltimore as a slave, Douglass would make his way into the city's free black community, in which he became an active member of the black Methodist Episcopal Church, taught reading and writing in black night schools and joined the East Baltimore Mental Improvement Society.

A THIRST FOR KNOWLEDGE

The move to Baltimore was a major turning point in Douglass' life. The eight-year-old slave, "once treated as a *pig* on the plantation . . . was treated as a *child* now." He was placed under the supervision of Auld's wife, Sophia, and charged with the responsibility of taking care of and protecting Tommy. Mrs. Auld was a "kindhearted" woman, and her influence on Douglass was significant. She quickly became a mother figure for Douglass as she recognized his humanity and treated him more like a son than a slave. In her presence, Douglass later recalled, "I could talk and sing; I could laugh and weep; I could reason and remember; I could love and hate. I was human, and she, dear lady, knew and felt me to be so."

Not only did Sophia Auld treat Douglass as a human being, she also stimulated in him an interest in language and in learning to read. "Mrs. Auld," Douglass recalled, "was not only a kind-hearted woman, but she was remarkably pious; frequent in her attendance of public worship, much given to reading the bible, and to chanting hymns when alone." Her habit of reading aloud from the Bible, he wrote, "awakened my curiosity in respect to this *mystery* of reading, and roused in me the desire to learn." One incident in particular appears to have had an especially powerful impact on Douglass in this regard. Later in his life, he recalled how he had fallen asleep one Sunday evening under the parlor table when he was awakened by the sound of Sophia Auld's voice, "mellow, loud, and sweet," reading Bible verses aloud from the book of Job. There was, for Douglass, enchantment in the way the words at once expressed beauty and despair. He was captivated by the manner in which Auld's voice made the words come alive from the printed page. "From that night," he recalled, "I date my thirst for knowledge." Moreover, Auld's tranquil voice empowered the young slave with the courage he needed to approach her to ask her to teach him to read. "Having no fear of my kind mistress," he recollected, "I frankly asked her to teach me to read; and without hesitation, the dear woman began the task."

Within a very short time Douglass was reading, and Mrs. Auld "seemed almost as proud" of his progress as if he had been "her own child." When she told her husband, however, that she was teaching the slave to read, he became extremely angry. Hugh Auld "at once forbade" her to instruct Douglass further. Reprimanding his wife in front of her pupil, Auld said:

> If you give a nigger an inch he will take an ell. Learning will spoil the best nigger in the world. If he learns to read the Bible it will forever unfit him to be a slave. He should know nothing but the will of his master, and learn to obey it. As to himself, learning will do him no good, but a great deal of harm, making him disconsolate and unhappy. If you teach him how to read, he'll want to know how to write, and this accomplished, he'll be running away with himself.

The "very decided manner" of Auld's lecture to his wife convinced Douglass that his master "was deeply sensible of the truths he was uttering." Convinced by Auld that literacy and learning were the paths out of slavery, Douglass was more determined than ever to acquire both. "In learning to read," Douglass wrote later, "I owe almost as much to the bitter opposition of my master, as to the kindly aid of my mistress. I acknowledge the benefit of both." Equally important, by denying Douglass access to a formal education, Hugh Auld inadvertently forced him to pursue a program of self-education that he would continue for the remainder of his life.

COLUMBIAN ORATOR

Of all Douglass' experiences in Baltimore, none had more impact than his discovery, at age twelve, of Caleb Bingham's *Columbian Orator.* Douglass was inspired to purchase the book when he overheard "some little boys say that they were going to learn some pieces out of it for the Exhibition." With fifty cents earned from polishing boots, he bought a copy of the reader. It was one of the best investments of his life. The *Columbian Orator* was a collection of orations, poems, playlets, and dialogues celebrating patriotism, freedom, courage, democracy, education, and temperance. Designed to "inspire the pupil with the ardour of eloquence and the love of virtue," the selections in the book were intended "particularly for Dialogue and Declamation."

"This volume was, indeed, a rich treasure," Douglass reflected in 1855, "and every opportunity afforded me, for a time, was spent in diligently perusing it." He found a number of pieces within the text particularly worthwhile. In his autobiographies, Douglass specifically mentioned Sheridan's "mighty speeches on the subject of Catholic Emancipation," Lord Chatham's speech "on the American War," and speeches by "the great William Pitt and by Fox" as addresses that he found particularly interesting. "These were all choice documents to me," Douglass recalled, "and I read them, over and over again, with an interest ever increasing because it was ever gaining in intelligence; for the more I read them, the better I understood them."

The selection he found most fascinating, however, was a short piece entitled "Dialogue Between a Master and Slave," by John Aikin. Douglass was so enamored of this dialogue that he "perused and reperused [it] with unflagging satisfaction." In *My Bondage and My Freedom*, Douglass explained the attraction of the dialogue, which began with the master rebuking the slave for attempting to escape. In response, the slave was "made to say some very smart as well as impressive things in reply to his master." Invited to defend his escape attempt, the slave accepted the challenge and made a "spirited defense of himself, and, thereafter the whole argument, for and against slavery, was brought out." For every argument the master made in defense of slavery, the slave presented a convincing counterargument. "The master," Douglass mused, "was vanquished at every turn." In the end, the master was convinced to emancipate the slave, demonstrating to Douglass the "mighty power and heart-searching directness of truth, penetrating even the heart of a slaveholder, compelling him to yield up his earthly interests to the claims of eternal justice." "Powerfully affected" by the dialogue, Douglass dreamed of the day "when the well-directed answers made by the slave to the master . . . would find their counterpart" in him.

WORDS TO EXPRESS HIS THOUGHTS

Equally important, Douglass stated years later, through reading and rereading this dialogue, he was able to utter his own thoughts on bondage, and "to meet the arguments brought forward to sustain slavery." Clearly and systematically, the dialogue responded to many of the questions that troubled him about slavery and his personal condition. Should he be grateful for his master's kind treatment of him? The dialogue's message was strikingly clear on this point. Douglass should not be grateful for any kind treatment by his owners who, if they did treat him well, did so purely for their own advantage. Was it wrong to try to escape from slavery? Decidedly not, said the dialogue. The act of running away was justified because the slave was taking back the liberty that was legitimately his. Had Providence, in some way, ordained slavery? Again, the dialogue answered—human beings, not God, had created slavery. From the dialogue, Douglass learned "the secret of all slavery and oppression, and . . . ascertained their true foundation to be in the pride, the power and the avarice of man." Slaveholders, he saw, were no more than "a band of successful robbers, who left their homes and went into Africa for the purpose of stealing and reducing my people to slavery."

Nor was this dialogue the only selection Douglass benefited from in the *Columbian Orator*. By reading Bingham's book "over and over again with unabated interest," he discovered the words to express his thoughts and feelings. The book, "gave tongue to interesting thoughts of my own soul," he recalled, thoughts "which had frequently flashed through my mind, and died away for want of utterance." He could now recite words that denounced slavery and injustice, that defended a slave's right to rebel and run away, and that celebrated human liberty and freedom. At the same time, he learned that words—and especially words expressed in oratory—could be a powerful way to combat such an injustice as slavery. According to one of the speeches found in Bingham's collection, the most telling weapon for truth was the art of oratory:

> To instruct, to persuade, to please; these are its objects. To scatter the clouds of ignorance and error . . . to remove the film of prejudice from the mental eye; and thus to irradiate the benighted mind with the cheering beams of troth. . . . An Alexander and a Caesar could conquer a world; but to overcome the passions, to subdue the wills, and to command at pleasure the inclinations of men, can be effected only by the all-powerful charm of enrapturing eloquence.

As Douglass read and reread the *Columbian Orator*, he recognized the possibilities of using oratory to "scatter the clouds of ignorance and error" that surrounded him in slave society.

Beyond showing Douglass the power of oratory and persuasive argument, Bingham's book provided a twenty-nine-page essay entitled, "General Directions for Speaking; Extracted from Various Authors." Within these pages Douglass found detailed instructions on how to deliver an effective speech, instructions he followed to the letter in many of his early antislavery addresses. Because it appears that Douglass' early rhetorical style and delivery were influenced profoundly by Bingham's essay, we need to look closely at its prescriptions.

RHETORICAL TACTICS

Bingham began his essay by declaring delivery the most important canon of rhetoric. Drawing upon the opinions of Cicero, Demosthenes, and Quintilian, he emphasized that the principal object of oratory was action, and that the primary trigger to action was the orator's manner of delivery. The most effective delivery, he advised, was natural and sincere. The orator must adjust his voice so that "it rises, sinks, and has various inflections given it, according to the present state and disposition of the mind." He must also attend to "accent, emphasis, and cadence." The orator must distinguish those words in a sentence which he believes are the "most important" and place "a greater stress of voice upon them than . . . upon the others." In addition, the speaker must speak loud enough to be heard. The voice, Bingham suggested, should be varied, "clear and distinct." Bingham also offered advice on the pacing of a speech. If the orator speaks too fast, he warned, he "destroys . . . the necessary distinction between sentence and sentence . . . by which mean, all the grace of speaking is lost, and in great measure, the advantage of hearing." Conversely, an orator who speaks too slowly "appears cool himself, [and] can never expect to warm his hearers, and excite their affections."

Like the voice, Bingham advised, gestures should be varied and natural. The orator should not stand in the same position "like a statue," but should move naturally about the platform. Bingham believed that the orator must use his face and eyes to show signs of sorrow, joy, anger, resentment, terror, and modesty. The eyes should always be "directed to some of the audience, and gradually turning from side to side with an air of respect and modesty, and looking at them decently in the face, as in common discourse." In addition, the speaker should stand erect and use "very moderate" hand and arm movements. Bingham also offered advice about imitating others from the platform, advice Douglass took seriously in his frequent use of mimicry in his early abolitionist lectures. An orator may choose to impersonate another speaker, wrote Bingham, but "great care must be taken not to overact his part by running into any ludicrous or theatrical mimicry."

Douglass learned from Bingham's book how to deliver each section of a speech. Upon arriving on the platform, the orator was directed to "first settle himself, compose his countenance, and take a respectful view of his audience." Once the audience was prepared to listen, the orator should begin his speech at a slow pace. Within the narration, "the voice ought to be raised to somewhat a higher pitch," though "matters of fact should be related in a very plain and distinct manner, with a proper stress and emphasis laid upon each circumstance." During the proposition, the "subject of the discourse should be delivered with a very clear and audible voice." Within the confirmation, speakers were instructed to use "a great variety both of the voice and gesture" so as to strengthen the orator's reasoning and heighten "the imagination of his hearers." During the confutation, "the arguments of the adverse party ought first to be repeated in a plain and distinct manner." If they appear "trifling and unworthy of a serious answer," instructed Bingham, the speaker should respond to them in a "facetious manner, both of expression and gesture," for "to attempt to answer, in a grave and serious manner, what is in itself empty and ludicrous, is apt to create a suspicion, of its having more in it than it really has." When coming to the conclusion, "both the voice and gesture should be brisk and sprightly. . . . If an enumeration of the principal arguments of the discourse be convenient . . . they ought to be expressed in the most clear and forcible manner." Bingham concluded his essay by stressing that "it is impossible to gain a just and decent pronunciation of voice and gesture merely from rules." The best way to become an orator, he recommended, was through "practice and imitation of the best examples." This may be one reason Douglass read the speeches, dialogues, playlets, and poems in the *Columbian Orator* "over and over again."

The importance of the *Columbian Orator* in shaping Douglass' future cannot be overestimated. Bingham's book offered him a heroic perspective of oratory, and a model for his own life that he appears to have found close to irresistible. Moreover, from all indications, Douglass' early oratory was influenced significantly by Bingham's meticulous instructions with respect to delivery, style, and arrangement. When speaking from the platform, Douglass used a conversational, natural delivery style, logically arranged and carefully reasoned his speeches, and appealed with great effect to the emotions of his listeners. Following Bingham's advice and reading and rereading the selections included in the book enabled Douglass to merge two traditions—the oral tradition of the slave culture with the classical rhetorical tradition. Since his childhood, he had absorbed the exhilarating oral style of the storyteller and slave preacher. He had been exposed to their use of striking imagery, rich phrases, metaphor, repetition, parallelism, poetry, song, and rhythmic cadences. He had experienced the impact of dramatic gestures and stirring vocal delivery on his fellow slaves. He had listened to the storyteller enhance his tale by mimicking the sounds of nature and by creating the illusion of dialogue between characters. Certainly, Bingham's advice on the orator's use of voice and gesture, mimicry and imagery, complemented the knowledge Douglass had acquired within his slave experiences on the plantation, as did Bingham's instructions on the importance of appealing to the emotions and passions of the audience. Most important, Bingham's volume introduced Douglass to the rhetorical strategies of the orator and to a standard structure for organizing speeches. Now armed with a formal introduction to rhetoric and with the words of the great orators of the past, he could meld his experiences within the slave community with the classical art of oratory. It was a potent combination, one that would leave white listeners agog at his eloquence and power as a platform orator throughout his public career.

CHAPTER 2

DOUGLASS AND THE ABOLITIONIST MOVEMENT

PEOPLE WHO MADE HISTORY

FREDERICK DOUGLASS

The Inevitability of the Douglass-Garrison Conflict

Tyrone Tillery

In his first decade as an antislavery activist, Frederick Douglass became involved with the American Anti-Slavery Society, an abolitionist group led by Boston reform journalist William Lloyd Garrison. In the early 1840s, Douglass loyally advocated the Garrisonian position that because the U.S. Constitution supported slavery, abolitionists should avoid compromising their cause by participation in the political system. During a two-year tour of Great Britain in the late 1840s, Douglass grew in intellectual self-confidence and when he returned to the United States he began a reassessment of the Constitution and politics. At the same time, he grew more resentful of the racially influenced paternalism of Garrison and many of his white abolitionist associates. Historian Tyrone Tillery, now at the University of Houston, concludes that tension between Douglass and Garrison was rooted in fundamental differences in personality as well as ideology and therefore Douglass's break from Garrison in the early 1850s was "inevitable."

From the founding of the American Anti-Slavery Society in 1833 abolitionism was marred by constant intra-group disagreements. Within seven years the movement split itself into two camps, one headed by William Lloyd Garrison and other commanded by such personalities as the Tappans, James G. Birney, Gerrit Smith and Joshua Leavitt. Ten years later another schism occurred which involved two groups disagreeing on proper tactics to employ in the abolition of slavery. The rupture of 1851 was the sole product of two per-

Tyrone Tillery, "The Inevitability of the Douglass-Garrison Conflict," *Phylon,* vol. 37, June 1976, pp. 137–45, 149. Copyright © 1976 by *Phylon:* The Atlanta University Review of Race and Culture. Reproduced by permission.

sonalities, William Lloyd Garrison and Frederick Douglass.

Studies of the Douglass-Garrison controversy have attributed the conflict to either the consequence of misunderstood events, beginning with the establishment of Douglass' *North Star* in 1847 and his subsequent betrayal of Garrisonian principles in 1851, or the result of the ambivalence of white abolitionists toward Negroes. . . . Both views are correct, but only as contributory factors. Closer examination of the conflict suggests that the split between Garrison and Douglass was inevitable. The conflict developed not from events beginning in 1847, but from circumstances which had created two individuals, each with his own personal needs, ideologies and ambitions.

Frederick Douglass' free life began sometime in September, 1838. But the exultant joy resulting from his new status was shortlived. He soon discovered, upon reaching New York, that even here he was not beyond the power of the slaveholders. Confused and unsure of anything except that "no man would ever have the right to call him slave, or assert mastery over him," Douglass sought refuge in a city where even black people would betray him for a few dollars. Finally, in desperation, Douglass confided in a sailor who put him in touch with David Ruggles, secretary of the New York Vigilance Committee. While hidden in Ruggles' office, Douglass was joined by his future wife, Anne. Twelve days later the two were married and moved to New Bedford, Massachusetts with only five dollars in his pocket.

But Douglass' financial situation did little to detract from the enthusiasm of being free. The privilege of freedom acted to stimulate Douglass' awareness of becoming his own man. In his words, "you may hurl a man so low, beneath the level of his kind, that he loses all just ideas of his natural position: but elevate him a little, and the clear conception of rights rises to life and power, and leads him onward." Freedom gave Douglass the clear conception he needed and by 1838 he was psychologically ready to become his own master.

Yet, while Douglass may have been psychologically ready to become his own master, in 1838 he had neither the ways nor the means to accomplish it. Still a fugitive, he was in constant danger of being recognized by pro-slavery men. And since slavery demanded the complete ignorance of its chattels for fear knowledge would teach them to throw off their yoke, Douglass had been denied the opportunity of a formal education. Nevertheless, the urgings for self-expression found Douglass seeking membership in the Methodist church. When he found that he could attend white Methodist churches only under humiliating conditions, he joined a small sect of his own race and soon became a leading member. Thus, early in Douglass' free life he learned the shortcomings of working in a white organization, a lesson that would be of immense value in his decision to start a Negro newspaper.

RECRUITED INTO ABOLITIONIST RANKS

But of all the avenues which afforded Douglass the opportunity to exploit his dormant powers of oratorical and intellectual expression, his introduction to the abolitionist movement *vis-a-vis* the Garrisonian wing was the most fruitful. Six months after reaching New Bedford he became a subscriber to Garrison's paper, and given Douglass' limited achievements in self-expression, the *Liberator* provided him the first opportunity to hear articulated those feelings he held toward the institution of slavery. In the words of Douglass,

> . . . Mr. Garrison, and his paper took a place in my heart second only to the Bible. It detested slavery, and made no truce with the traffickers in the bodies and souls of men. It preached human brotherhood, it exposed hypocrisy and wickedness in high places: it denounced oppression, and with all the solemnity of "Thus saith the Lord," demanded complete emancipation of my race. He seemed to me, an all-sufficient match for every opponent, whether they spoke in the name of the law or the gospel. His words were full of holy fire, and straight to the point.

For seven years following his introduction to Garrison in 1839, Douglass would echo the Garrisonian principles and philosophy. In the capacity of a lecturer, a title which meant little more than the discriptive narration of his life as a slave, Douglass was invited to join the Massachusetts Anti-Slavery Society. As the prize exhibit Douglass traveled with other abolitionists telling the story of his slave experiences. . . .

CONDESCENSION TOWARD DOUGLASS

For some time the Garrisonians failed to see that Douglass' talents lay not in his being an escaped slave but in a wide range of abilities. But events rapidly illustrated how seriously he had been underrated. The winter and spring of 1842 found Douglass stumping through eastern and central

Massachusetts in the company of Garrison, Samuel J. May, Charles Remond and the Hutchinsons, a musically self-trained family that sang anti-slavery songs. It is significant that on this tour Douglass had not only aroused enthusiasm but made color enviable. Writing to Garrison from North-bridge, a veteran abolitionist observed, "It has been my fortune to hear a great many anti-slavery lecturers and many distinguished speakers on other subjects: but it has rarely been my lot to listen to one whose power over me was greater than Douglass', and not over me only, but over all who heard him. . . ."

Douglass' rapid development as a brilliant thinker and orator had caused much concern among his abolitionist friends. Instead of being proud that this former Negro slave had been able in a short time to equal and even surpass many of the white spokesmen against slavery, they were worried by it and even resented it. In a few years Douglass would become fully aware that jealously, power and envy could take priority over principles.

TASTING GREATER FREEDOM IN EUROPE

Despite the resentment on the part of the Boston Garrisonians, Douglass continued to develop his talents, both as an orator and as a writer. With the publication of his *Narrative of the Life of Frederick Douglass* in 1845, Douglass had proven beyond a doubt that here was a man of extraordinary talents. When he departed for his first trip abroad in the same year, people could only echo Wendell Phillips when he said, "If you ever see him, Remember that in my opinion, you see the most remarkable and by far the ablest colored man we have ever had here." It is reported that Phillips told Douglass to be himself and he would succeed; but as Phillip Foner put it, "Not even Phillips dreamed that success would reach such heights. His European visit gave Douglass international reputation. He returned to the States a world figure, a mighty power for freedom."

Barring a few unpleasantries on board the *Cambria*, Douglass' trip to England was an unqualified success. Not only had the reception by the English people been over-whelming, but the stay in England provided Douglass with the intellectual and physical growing room heretofore denied him in America. For the first time Douglass was exposed to a wide range of reform movements. Initially Douglass resisted the lure of the new intellectual freedom, but soon he became convinced that it was impossible to divide the struggle against oppression into separate compartments. In one of Douglass' most prophetic remarks he explained to Garrison,

> . . . though I am more closely connected and identified with one class of outrage, oppressed and enslaved people, I cannot allow myself to be insensible to the wrongs and sufferings of any part of the great family of man. I am not only an American slave, but a man, and as such, am bound to use my powers for the welfare of the whole human brotherhood.

Undoubtedly, the spirit of freedom in the British Isles had influenced Douglass' thinking not only on American slavery but also on a variety of other subjects. He was especially impressed in Ireland by what he called "the spirit of freedom that seems to animate all with whom I come in contact—and the entire absence of everything that looked like prejudice against me, on account of the color of my skin—contrasting so strongly with my long and bitter experience in the United States, that I look with wonder and amazement on the transition."

The influence had become evident following a second confrontation with Maria Chapman, leader of the Boston Female Anti-Slavery Society. On this occasion she had impugned Douglass' integrity by cautioning Richard Webb, an Irish abolitionist, to keep an eye on Douglass, "lest he might be bought up by the London committee." As if symbolic of the change which had occurred in him, Douglass sharply rebuked Maria Chapman for her insinuations and threatened to leave the Anti-Slavery Society if its members attempted to supervise his activities. . . .

BREAKING TIES WITH THE GARRISONIANS

Of all the events that seemed to herald the split between Douglass and Garrison, none could have been more symbolic than the purchase of Douglass' freedom by his English friends late in 1846. Considerable resentment and disappointment was voiced against it by his abolitionist friends, as they had come to believe that the purchase was tacit recognition of the "right to traffic in human beings." Typical of such feelings was a statement by Henry C. Wright in a letter addressed to Douglass:

> I cannot bear to think of you as being a party to such trans-

actions, even by silence. If others will take that paper and keep it as an evidence of your freedom, you cannot prevent them, but I wish you would see it your duty, publicly to disown the deed, and never to recognize that hateful Bill!

He also added that if Douglass refused he would never write him again. In vain Douglass tried to explain to his abolitionist friends that his acceptance of the transaction was justified in light of what he termed the distinction between "natural freedom" and "legal freedom." His purchase only satisfied the legal freedom requirement.

Nevertheless, Douglass returned to America a free man. His tour in England had firmly established him not only as the premier speaker for black people, but also as an important spokesman for the abolitionist movement. Before departing, Douglass had been offered a substantial sum of money for the purpose of starting his own paper. But again Douglass met opposition from the Garrisonians. Garrison argued that there were already in existence a number of Negro journals, hence there would be no surprise attached to the appearance of a periodical handled ably by a colored man. Besides,

William Lloyd Garrison

it was doubtful that Douglass would be able to secure enough subscriptions. Garrison also suggested that a venture into journalism would destroy his status as a lecturer. Douglass retreated and temporarily put aside his plans for publication. However, a number of letters poured into the *Liberator* expressing regret that he had decided to postpone his venture. Many letters went so far as to accuse Douglass' opponents of fear. For example, one letter exclaimed, "those who fear that Mr. Douglass' editorial duties would withdraw him from the field as a lecturer would do well to remember that the editor of the *Liberator* devoted much time to lecturing in parts of the country, and his editorials are none the less prompt, spirited and plentiful." One letter to Garrison predicted that if published Douglass' paper would "within one year have a greater subscription list than any other anti-slavery paper." And it continued, "is it possible that you and others are fearful that the *Liberator* and the *Standard* will suffer in consequence?"

Douglass published an unconvincing statement denying that he had been coerced by the "Boston Board." But within a month the *Anti-Slavery Standard* announced Douglass would become a permanent columnist for the paper.

Douglass had acquiesced, but not for long; by October rumors spread that he had decided to start his newspaper in Cleveland. However, on November 5, 1847 the *Liberator* announced Douglass was establishing the *North Star* in Rochester. Douglass had decided the time had come for him to rely on his own abilities, proved and potential. Furthermore, he had resolved that a journal excellently managed and edited by a Negro would be a powerful evidence that Negroes were too much men to be chattels. Douglass' reversal of his earlier decision angered many of his abolitionist colleagues; but none was more vexed than Garrison, who considered Douglass' conduct about the paper "highly inconsistent with his decision in Boston." Garrison's accusation seemed based more on fear than on fact. Early in 1847 two incidents aroused his suspicions of Douglass' loyalty. The first happened during his tour with Douglass soon after Douglass returned from Europe. The hardships encountered on the trip, rain, malarial weather, and crowded engagements, had physically drained Garrison. He took ill on September 13, and could not continue with the tour. Douglass offered to remain with his co-worker but Garrison urged he go on with the tour. When learning that Garrison's condition had deteriorated Douglass reproached himself for leaving him. Slowly Garrison recuperated and accused Douglass of not being concerned about his health, apparently ignoring a letter from Samuel May describing Douglass' sorrow and suspense over his illness. Perhaps Garrison had become uneasy over the recent sentiments drawn up in a meeting held by black people of Philadelphia honoring Douglass and Garrison. The sentiment had proclaimed Douglass "the stanch advocate of Liberty in which time could never erase the memory of so great a champion." Garrison, on the other hand, had only been proclaimed the "first to cry hold to the tyrants of the South."

With the establishment of the *North Star* Garrison was sure Douglass' actions reflected "pure infidelity." Undeterred by Garrison's attitude, Douglass continued to publish his paper, and Garrison's disappointment did not prevent him from permitting his paper to praise the new weekly. In fact, on numerous occasions Garrison's paper had reprinted articles by Douglass supporting a particular view on slavery. Douglass kept in contact with Garrison, often lauding Garrison's achievements to the movement. He and Garrison frequently met at the annual meetings of the American Anti-Slavery Society; but the old camaraderie was gone, and after 1851 the relationship was in shambles. At that time Douglass publicly announced a fundamental change in his political views.

DIFFERING VIEWS ON THE CONSTITUTION

Since Douglass joined the abolitionist movement he had endorsed the basic theories of the Garrisonian school. One such theory involved Garrison's view of the Constitution and politics. The Constitution, as Garrison saw it, was a pro-slavery document. And after 1844 the Garrisonians resolved to be non-political and non-voting to insure "No Union with the Slaveholders." As editor of the *North Star,* Douglass' views on the subject gradually underwent a change. Being away from the scrutinizing eyes of the "Boston Board" gave him the opportunity to observe what other Anti-Slavery men were doing. The impact of this freedom to independently explore other schools of thought was reflected in Douglass' ideas on the Constitution. By March, 1848, Douglass had clearly exhibited signs of confusion and uncertainty as to the true nature of the Constitution. In the *North Star* he argued, "that the Constitution of the United States, standing alone and construed only in the light of its letter without reference to the opinions of the men who framed and adopted it, or to the uniform universal and undeviating practice of the nation under it, from the time of its adoption until now is not a pro-slavery instrument." He did however, qualify his statement by pointing out that it did contain features which supported slavery.

Douglass' comments on the Constitution in 1848 were not the only signs of a radical departure in Garrisonian principles. Frequently Douglass had shown interest in anti-slavery political parties. In June, 1847 he attended the National Liberty Party convention in Buffalo and the next year supported it in the *North Star.* He praised the Liberty Party for giving merits to black people. Later that year he also gave credit to the Free Soil Party as a challenge to the slaveholding parties during the Wilmot Proviso escapade. As Douglass saw it: "The intelligence, moral worth and philanthropy and numerical strength assumed by this party makes it our duty to inquire what courses those who stand forth as friends of the slave ought to pursue towards that Party."

Furthermore, Douglass added, the Liberty Party supported many of the same goals as the abolitionists. Like the abolitionists they believed Congress should abolish slavery wherever they possessed the constitutional powers to do so and to free the government from all responsibility for slavery by abolishing all slave trade and declaring no more slave states or slavery in the territories. While Douglass had not relinquished his belief that moral reform should be regarded as the real anti-slavery tactic in favor of anti-slavery political groups, he had arrived at the conclusion that it was his duty to pursue any course which would make anti-slavery advocates, in some degree, a terror to evil-doers.

Step by step Douglass came to believe that the Constitution was not a pro-slavery document and that there was no need to dissolve the Union. He had now substituted Garrison's "No union with slaveholders" for his "No union with slaveholding." At the eighteenth annual meeting of the American Anti-Slavery Society held in Syracuse in May, 1851, Douglass shocked the Garrisonian abolitionists by opposing a proposition not to support any newspaper that did not assume the Constitution to be a pro-slavery document. Douglass protested that the Constitution "might be consistent in its details with the noble purpose avowed in its preamble." Immediately Garrison exclaimed, "there is roguery somewhere," and moved to have the *North Star* stricken from the list; and this was promptly done by the convention. In one instant Douglass had become a heretic.

THE RELATIONSHIP'S END

In vain Douglass denied he had become a renegade. Shortly, accusations that his change in political views was due more to his recent merger with the Liberty Party Paper than a sincere conversion came from Garrison's friends. After the initial accusations, issues ceased being the center of the controversy and verbal warfare ensued between Douglass and his opponents. The verbal conflagration reached its height when Garrison insinuated Douglass was having an affair with Julia Griffiths, Douglass' white secretary. Between Douglass and Garrison the die had been cast and the split was now complete. . . .

The Douglass-Garrison split aptly illustrated that history rarely operates in black and white contrasts, but in a series of varying grays. The conflict had been the result of not one but a number of subtle causes which neither Douglass nor Garrison could control. It was not only the result of misunderstanding and paternalism, but personality and ideological differences derived from vastly different experiences creating individuals whose needs would eventually run a collision course. The events following 1847 were anticlimatic; the die had been cast years before Douglass and Garrison had met in New Bedford, Massachusetts. Circumstances of birth, of color, of doctrines and philosophy had conspired to make the conflict between Garrison and Douglass inevitable.

Frederick Douglass, Preacher

William L. Andrews

William L. Andrews, the E. Maynard Adams Professor
of English at University of North Carolina at Chapel
Hill, is the preeminent scholar of the slave narrative
and related forms of antebellum African American
autobiography. In the essay excerpted below, Andrews examines Douglass's claim in his two pre–
Civil War autobiographies that he had been a lay
minister. Andrews locates contemporary accounts
verifying that Douglass served as a class-leader in
congregations of the small African Methodist Episcopal Zion Church first in Maryland and later in Massachusetts. Andrews argues that it was Douglass's experience speaking in those black churches that gave
him the self-confidence and oratorical skills to become one of the greatest abolitionist orators.

As scholarly interest increases in Frederick Douglass as a
man of letters, the vagueness of his literary origins becomes
increasingly frustrating to those who wish to trace the intellectual background of the author of America's classic slave
autobiography. In the *Narrative of the Life of Frederick Douglass* (1845) and in *My Bondage and My Freedom* (1855),
Douglass gives priority in his early intellectual development
to *The Columbian Orator*, an eloquence manual and anthology of speeches, which he bought when he was about twelve
or thirteen years old. In addition to teaching him anti-
slavery arguments, this volume may well have pointed
Douglass in the direction of oratory as his mode, and
polemics as his sphere, of public expression. However, while
a teenager in Baltimore, young Frederick Bailey also read
and copied from the Bible, a Methodist hymnbook, an un-
specified Webster's spelling book, "and other books which

had accumulated on my hands". Equally important to his evolving sense of his destiny as an orator was the advice that thirteen-year-old Frederick received from a man he called "Father Lawson," a black Baltimore drayman to whom the youth had become "deeply attached." Lawson told his protégé "that he had been shown that I must preach the gospel." Because this pious old man had become Frederick's "spiritual father," "his words made a deep impression on my mind, and I verily felt that some such work was before me."

ASPIRING LAY PREACHER

In slavery Douglass had little opportunity to pursue a preaching career. A member of white Methodist congregations in Baltimore and St. Michael's, Maryland, since 1831, he found opportunities "in which to exercise my gifts" only when he involved himself in sub rosa Sabbath schools for blacks. On Thomas Auld's plantation in 1833 and again on William Freeland's farm in 1835, Douglass took leadership roles in clandestine religious institutions designed to teach slaves to read the Bible. Each of these short-lived schools was forcibly dissolved by panicky slaveholders, but not before they had influenced the young teacher profoundly. In the second school, which Douglass founded and conducted entirely on his own, he experienced a greater sense of common purpose and emotional solidarity with other blacks than he had ever felt before. He wrote in 1855: "I have had various employments during my short life; but I look back to *none* with more satisfaction, than to that afforded by my Sunday school."

It is not surprising, therefore, that after having been jim-crowed at the altar of a white Methodist church in New Bedford, Massachusetts, a few months after his escape from slavery, Douglass united with "a small body of colored Methodists, known as the Zion Methodists." No doubt his experience as the head of a black Sunday school in the South had something to do with his being "soon made a class-leader and a local preacher" among the Zion Methodists. The fact that Douglass's first public speaking in the North was religious in nature and for black congregations is something that he first specified in *My Bondage and My Freedom.* In the memorable climax to the *Narrative,* he refers vaguely to his having spoken "in the colored people's meeting at New Bedford" before addressing whites for the first time at a Nantucket anti-slavery

convention in August, 1841. But critics have ignored the prece-
dence of preaching over polemics in the evolution of Douglass's self-concept as man speaking. The language and structure of the *Narrative*'s conclusion invite the reader to see the
ex-slave before the Nantucket abolitionists as "a man . . . first
finding his voice and then, as sure as light follows dawn,
speaking 'with considerable ease.'"

PREACHER BEFORE ABOLITIONIST

We may never know to what extent and in what ways Douglass found his voice as a black preacher among the Zion
Methodists before he began to make his fame addressing
white anti-slavery audiences. However, we can document his
situation in this all-black church in more detail than has previously been brought out. Douglass's preaching role among
the Zion Methodists was attested in the *Wonderful Eventful
Life of Rev. Thomas James* (1804–1891), the narrative of a
black Rochester, New York, clergyman active in the anti-
slavery movement. James recalls Douglass as a member of
the New Bedford Zion Methodists in 1840, the year James
took charge of the church. Douglass "had been given authority to act as an exhorter by the church before my coming,"
wrote James, "and I some time afterwards licensed him to
preach. . . . On one occasion, after I had addressed a white
audience on the slavery question, I called upon Fred. Douglass, whom I saw among the auditors, to relate his story. He
did so, and in a year from that time he was in the lecture field
with Parker Pillsbury and other leading abolitionist orators."
Since James provides no specifics about this occasion, it is
impossible to determine the accuracy of this anecdote or to
tell whether this black minister, not the white abolitionist
William C. Coffin, was actually the first to steer Frederick
Douglass into anti-slavery oratory. At any rate, James's recollections concur with Douglass's autobiography in showing
him a preacher before he was a polemicist, while also suggesting how the obscure black preacher in New Bedford
could have found his way to the abolitionist platform.

The Radical as Reformer

Leslie Friedman Goldstein

In the following selection, Leslie Friedman Goldstein, the Judge Hugh M. Morris Professor of Political
Science at the University of Delaware and prolific
author on issues of constitutional law, analyzes the
political philosophy of Frederick Douglass. She finds
that Douglass switched from the Garrisonian abolitionists' rejection of nonviolent revolutionary change
of American values when he became convinced that
there were no constitutional barriers to antislavery
political reform. Entering the political arena, however, did not lead Douglass to compromise his radical goal of immediate emancipation for all slaves. In
the 1850s, Douglass actively prodded the Free Soil
and Republican parties to adopt a more stringent
abolitionist stance but ultimately endorsed their candidates as the best available to the antislavery voter.
Goldstein concludes that through such tactics, Douglass found a way to maintain high moral standards
while still having a significant impact on the mainstream party system.

Frederick Douglass—more by virtue of his influence as a
journalist, orator, author, and Republican party activist than
because of any government offices he held—deserves to be
considered an outstanding black American statesman of the
latter half of the nineteenth century. As one of America's most
thoughtful statesmen, he pondered at considerable length the
tension between pure morality, on the one hand, and political feasibility, on the other. He saw that the statesman needs
not only ethical but practical wisdom, for what is politically
practicable may not be purely good in the abstract ethical
sense. Frederick Douglass, it seems, felt this tension more in-

Leslie Friedman Goldstein, "Morality & Prudence in the Statesmanship of Frederick
Douglass: Radical as Reformer," *Polity*, vol. 16, Summer 1984, pp. 606–23. Copyright
© 1984 by *Polity*: The Journal of the Northeastern Political Science Association. Reproduced by permission.

tensely than most other American statesmen did; certainly he spoke and wrote about it more frequently than most.

The social evils that Douglass targeted for attack were overwhelming in their enormity. He confronted not only the enslavement of millions of blacks with the acquiescence of the white majority, but also confronted widespread denials to free blacks of the right to vote and to bear arms. As a member of this powerless minority struggling against the wrongdoing of the politically and economically powerful majority, Douglass faced a conflict between morality and prudence that was posed about as sharply as it can be posed for a statesman. His thoughtful analysis of this perennial dilemma should be of interest to all those who may be concerned with improving the status of an oppressed minority within a political system that pays heed to majority will. . . .

POLITICS AND MORALITY

Frederick Douglass became a political activist virtually as soon as he escaped from slavery in 1837. That is, he became a public agitator against the institution of slavery. But in the beginning he did not understand his own activity to be "political." He knew that he intended to reform public opinion in order to persuade Americans to outlaw slavery, but he viewed this as a moral *rather* than as a political crusade. He associated "politics" with the greedy quest for the material fruits of public office, and insisted that religion, not politics, sustains slavery in that it forms the community's morals and molds men's consciences. Douglass called Americans to a "higher and holier warfare" than that they would find on the battlefield of political action, and warned against the corrupting lures of the political arena. Instead, Douglass put his hopes in the press and pulpit for the moral education of America.

Apparently as a result of contacts with such abolitionists as John Brown, as well as from listening to, and engaging in, the debates between the Garrisonian Abolitionists (who opposed political action) and the voting-oriented Political Abolitionists over whether the Constitution was proslavery or antislavery, Douglass came gradually to an appreciation of the possibility of bringing about moral and social reform *through* politics. In the process he changed his view of the nature of politics itself. He came to realize that the political task is not simply to acquire the power of office but that politics is, properly speaking, a moral endeavor. It is concerned with establishing justice and advancing the common good. Douglass surpassed even his post-Garrisonian mentor, Gerrit Smith, in his new understanding of the moral dimension of politics. In August of 1851, shortly after abandoning the Garrisonian stand *contra* political participation, he wrote to Smith:

> I cannot agree with you . . . in respect to the bounds you set to government. . . . I have a notion that the state—not less than the church should cover the whole ground of morals—incorporating into itself all great moral truths—if government were *righteous* government, there could be little objection to committing education . . . to its charge.

Douglass went on to argue repeatedly throughout his later career that political leadership, no less than religious leadership, must address the moral life of the citizenry, and that the function of laws was not only to coerce but also to educate the people. He made statements to this effect both in theoretical analyses of the nature of law and political leadership, and in analytic descriptions of the Civil War and Reconstruction and post-Reconstruction conflicts. Moral issues, Douglass came firmly to believe, were the very stuff of politics; it was "good versus evil, right versus wrong, liberty versus slavery."

Even at his most anti-political, however, Douglass had never endorsed the philosophical anarchism of his earliest mentor, William Lloyd Garrison. Garrison and the members of his Non-Resistance Society regarded the use of *all* force, even the force of lawful government, as morally wrong. Douglass never precluded the use of government force against evils such as slavery. What had attracted Douglass to the Garrisonian school, at first, was not its philosophy but its persuasive interpretation of the American Constitution. Douglass distinguished sharply between lawful and lawless force, arguing that a government that violated its fundamental charter would be "nothing better than a lawless mob, acting without any higher authority than its own impulses or convictions." The nature of the Constitution, embodying the fundamental principles of the regime, was then the pivot on which turned the answers to the most basic of political questions: whether to be a reformer or a revolutionary.

REFORM VERSUS REVOLUTION

Indeed, Douglass characterizes this question as *the* point of controversy between the two abolitionist camps. When he changed over to the Voting Abolitionist camp in 1851, he designated his new position as "one of reform, not of revolution." Paradoxical as it seems, he accompanied this rejection of (non-violent) revolution with a new acceptance of violence as a tactic. In other words, Douglass turned away from the posture of a non-violent revolutionary toward that of a reformer accepting the need for violence. . . .

Douglass' overall strategy can be simply stated: Do not burden yourself with more than is necessary and use all the legitimate weapons available. If the fundamental law of the land overtly, and in its dominant spirit, opposes a direly needed social reform, and would not admit of amendment to the contrary, then the inescapable obligation of a just man is to advocate revolutionary change. He must then agitate for a new fundamental law that would establish the regime on a more just foundation. If, however, the basic principles of the regime, as enunciated in its fundamental law, do not oppose the needed reform and do allow political means for enacting it, it is clearly preferable to work within the law. Public opinion must be moved to support the reform, and the law is a powerful vehicle for moving public opinion.

Thus, Douglass argued that, "the great gulf between voting and nonvoting abolitionists" had developed from disagreement over whether or not the Constitution was pro-slavery. His changed perception of the Constitution—from the view that it was a pro-slavery document in intent and in legal content to the one that it was anti-slavery in both respects—greatly influenced how he weighed the slavery elements of the American regime against the freedom-favoring elements. . . .

Indeed, so convinced was Douglass of the usefulness of having the Constitution on his side, that he stopped characterizing it as *pro*-slavery months before he became convinced that it was *anti*-slavery. He would rather be silent than hand over the Constitution on a silver platter to his enemies. Douglass' perception of the Constitution eventually changed when he recognized that deliberate omissions of words must be taken into account in interpreting documents, considered the Constitution's own wording, saw that the founders expected slavery soon to end under the Constitution, and realized that slavery had been much weaker during the early years of the Republic than it had been in recent decades. Douglass then began to call for political action, for change *within* the existing political system, to end slavery.

As soon as Douglass could honestly convince himself—and this took him at least two years of careful study—that the basic principles of the American regime could be viewed as supporting, or even requiring, the abolition of slavery, he happily cast off the additional burden of overthrowing the whole American government. He began to argue that the political and legal principles on which this country stood could not tolerate the continuation of slavery.

The political and historical circumstances in which Douglass was operating made revolutionary solutions problematic. While it is generally simpler to change a particular social institution than to destroy and reconstitute an entire government, the Garrisonian revolutionary option—which was the major abolitionist alternative during the pre–Civil War years—made matters worse by urging secession. The Garrisonians not only denounced the Constitution but also asked that the Union be split into at least two fragments so that the morally pure need have "no union with slaveholders."

The longer Douglass pondered the secession solution the less workable he found it to be. By 1855, the prospect of massive slave escapes or revolts, even if the North left the Union and encouraged them, appeared remote. It followed that breaking the Union because of opposition to slavery would leave the slaves to their masters. Southern slave-masters would remain as untroubled by American abolitionists as were the slaveholders of Brazil and Cuba. To counsel *this* kind of overthrow of the government would not only place added burdens upon the abolitionist cause; it would practically result in abandoning the goal of abolition.

ABOLITION ABOVE ALL OTHER REFORMS

Douglass' strategy of avoiding unnecessary burdens in attaining the desired reform may seem to be inconsistent with his active involvement in a wide array of other reform movements—temperance, Irish Liberation, opposition to capital punishment, women's rights. From a lifetime perspective, however, his participation in these movements was of secondary importance. Even the women's rights movement, for which he worked throughout his adult life, did not distract him from his primary commitment.

Douglass had a sharply delineated set of priorities. None of the social evils against which he campaigned could approximate the horrors of slavery, and he made this explicit from the start. He noted, for example, in 1846:

> It is common . . . to distinguish every bad thing by the name of slavery. Intemperance is slavery; to be deprived of the right to vote is slavery, says one; to have to work hard is slavery, says another. . . .
>
> I do not wish for a moment to detract from the horror with which the evil of intemperance is contemplated—not at all; nor do I wish to throw the slightest obstruction in the way of any political freedom that any class of persons in this country may desire to obtain. But I am here to say that I think the term slavery is sometimes abused by identifying it with that which it is not.

Just as he himself put the abolition of slavery—because of the incomparable evils of that institution—above all other social reforms in significance and urgency, so he expected other American abolitionists to do the same. He had no sympathy for the women abolitionists who allowed themselves, in his view, to be carried away by their own desire for equal status to such an extent that they would split the American Anti-Slavery Society over the issue of the treatment of its women members. Similarly, Douglass was disappointed with the leaders of the feminist Equal Rights Association (Lucy Stone, Elizabeth Cady Stanton, and Susan B. Anthony) when they refused to endorse the Fifteenth Amendment on the grounds of its failure to give the vote to women. Douglass was willing to continue to work separately for the cause of black suffrage and for the cause of women's suffrage, but he was not willing to have them merged into a single cause. That would have increased the odds against public acceptance of the suffrage package; "all or nothing" was decidedly not Douglass' strategy as a reformer.

This is not to say that he refrained from advocating drastic and radical reforms; the point is that he was willing to push for them one at a time. The abolition of slavery was a radical change and so was the granting of suffrage to freed men who had been out of slavery for only five years. Douglass labored hard for each of these, but he did not insist that the former was not worth taking if the latter were not simultaneously granted. True to this pattern, he returned to participation in the women's suffrage movement *after* the Fifteenth Amendment had been adopted. . . .

It should be emphasized that Douglass' preference for

taking first things first did not imply an acceptance of "gradualism" as a reform strategy. Justice being his measure, and confronted as he was with " monstrous iniquity" in his own homeland, he spoke proudly of his "radical opinions" and his "ultraist" behavior. He did not shy away from the fact that, as an abolitionist, he was calling for a genuinely radical transformation of the American social system.

Not only did Douglass have radical goals, he favored radical measures for attaining those goals. His preference for drastic or shocking tactics was linked to his concern with reshaping public opinion. Drastic tactics—on *either* side—served to awaken public interest. Once people started paying attention, Douglass believed, the evils of slavery would, as it were, speak for themselves.

> I like radical measures, whether adopted by Abolitionists or slaveholders. . . . I am delighted to see any effort to prop up the system on the part of the slaveholders. It serves to bring up the subject before the people, and hasten the day of deliverance.

This, of course, was the basic reasoning behind "agitation" as a reform method; the public mind should be agitated to the point where it would recognize the horrors of slavery. Because America was a democratic republic, once public opinion favored the abolition of slavery, the battle would be won.

PARTIES AND POLITICIANS

Douglass' entry into the fray of party politics did not moderate his interest in the radical or the extreme measure. He viewed his activities in party politics as simply another segment of his overall effort to move public sentiment toward the abolitionist position. His efforts in party politics were really a series of attempts to radicalize the party conflict. He wished the electoral conflict to center around the most fundamental issues facing the regime. In a letter written before the war, he observed: "We have turned Whigs and Democrats into Republicans, and we can turn Republicans into Abolitionists."

As a radical agitator, Douglass welcomed the extremism, the aggressive audacity, of the proslavery forces. Measures such as the Congressional "gag rule," the infamous declaration of Judge [Roger B.] Taney that Negroes had no rights in America, the display of brute force within the very halls of Congress, the bloody battle over Kansas—all these, according to Douglass, "served as fuel to the fire" which was heating the nation toward the conflagration that would put an end to slavery. Douglass gave the brazen Kansas-Nebraska Act, and its cavalier repeal of the Missouri Compromise, the credit for having brought Abraham Lincoln onto the national political scene, and for having convinced Northern public opinion that the slavery question was no longer "to be slighted or ignored. . . ."

Despite this preference for radical improvements in the existing polity, Douglass understood it to be an axiom of electoral politics that a party must have "not only ideas, but numbers." He recognized that the degree of compromise, or of moderation of principles, suitable to party action was of necessity different from the level of compromise appropriate for a personal morality. He explained the distinction as follows:

> There is a place in the world for individual action, and a place for political party action. In the field of moral action, a man may place his standard as high as he pleases. In this field, one man with the right and the true is a majority. He may invoke his standard of religious perfection . . . but in politics a man to be of any practical use to his country or the world, must work with the multitudes.

Any political party, if it meant to have an impact, could not appeal only to a moral elite; it would have to be able to attract a majority or a near-majority of the voters. (A near majority might pose enough of a threat that the other party would be influenced to change its stance on crucial issues). This interpretation of the role of morals in party politics in a democracy came to Douglass gradually. A chronological retracing of his involvement in the American party system illustrates the dilemma he confronted as a radical reformer attempting to influence electoral politics.

Douglass perceived the potential of the ballot as a weapon for social change long before he actually entered the political battlefield. This first phase of his involvement with politics might be seen as a period of intensely interested ambivalence. His views on the Constitution pulled him in one direction; his interest in politics, in another. From 1848, when the controversy over the Wilmot Proviso gave birth to the Free Soil Party, until Douglass openly abandoned Garrisonianism in 1851, he belied his own principled rejection of participation in party conflict by his editorial support for, and his active personal involvement in, both the Liberty Party and the Free Soil Party Conventions.

During this phase Douglass personally opposed voting

because he still believed that the Constitution was pro-
slavery (and that therefore any elected official would be
sworn to uphold slavery), but he praised the Free Soil Party
for publicizing the antislavery cause and for giving an anti-
slavery option to those who (mistakenly) believed in voting.
He endorsed the Free Soil candidates in the manner of a
physician who concedes that cigars will harm the patient
less than cigarettes. Douglass himself maintained Garrisonian purity and refused to vote, but he advised his politically
active readers that a Free Soil vote would be a lesser evil
than contributing to the extension of slavery.

Both his praise and his criticism of the Free Soil campaign
of 1848 indicate that Douglass saw that party's value as agitational rather than electoral. He credited it with rallying
new members to the anti-slavery cause, and with teaching a
lesson to certain recalcitrant politicians. He was disappointed, however, with its watering down of the abolitionist
doctrine. For, by its willingness to compromise for the sake
of winning allies, the party had muddied the former clarity
of the Abolitionist position and confused the public.

> Upon the whole it has left the public mind in a more difficult
> state to deal with than it found it. It found it agitated, divided,
> and the lines drawn distinctly but has left it dull, stupid, un-
> defined, and indifferent. Instead of making the task of the
> abolitionist lighter, it has increased his burdens. . . .

However, some of his statements show that [the] matter of
providing anti-slavery voters a vehicle to express their view-
point was not so important to Douglass as his expectation
that this anti-slavery party would eventually lead to an even
more radically anti-slavery party. The problem was that the
more people the Free Soil Party tried to represent, the more
diluted and nebulous its anti-slavery principles became. As
its electoral chances improved, its educational or agitational
role declined. Douglass watched sadly as, in 1849, the Free
Soil Party admitted Democrats into its ranks. His comment at
this time presents an interesting contrast to his more mature
views on the need for compromise in politics quoted above.

> Why should Free Soilers wish to unite with any party, on any
> basis, were it not from some such motive [of expediency]?
> Two or three are sufficient to make a party, if a party must be
> made; one is sufficient to stand alone if he is only satisfied of
> the truth of his principles.

During the years 1848–1851, Douglass stayed aloof from

politics by refusing to vote, and in this way paid his obeisance to moral principle. He also paid his tribute to numbers by endorsing the Free Soil candidates for the 1848 election. For the 1852, 1856, and 1860 elections, Douglass developed a new position to cope with the numbers vs. principle dilemma. He stayed outside the Free Soil and then the Republican Party until late in the campaigns, claimed to be a member of the Liberty or Radical Abolitionist Party (a very small group mostly in New York), and denounced the Free Soilers (and later the Republicans) for not being sufficiently anti-slavery. In this way, he upheld the anti-slavery principles, and tried to move the more mainstream party toward his preferred position. However, each time, shortly before the election, Douglass shifted his ground and endorsed the more mainstream party candidates (Free Soil in 1852 and Republican in 1856 and 1860). These shifts in August of 1852 and 1856 and in October of 1860 indicate that Douglass would not altogether reject practical wisdom in favor of moral fervor. He knew that numbers do count in elections and that the results of elections could do great harm or considerable good to the slave's cause.

Douglass persisted in this in-again-out-again pattern, instead of remaining within the Free Soil or Republican Party, perhaps because he believed that he could influence the party more as an outside agitator than as a member of its organization. It is conceivable that his formal membership in the party would have been viewed as a tacit endorsement of Free Soil, rather than Radical Abolitionist, principles.

The dramatic transformation of Abraham Lincoln, from a presidential candidate only moderately anti-slavery to the president who emancipated the slaves, seems to have profoundly altered Douglass' attitude toward political parties. Convinced now of the importance of winning elections, and indelibly impressed with the fact that the Republican Party had freed four million of his oppressed brethren, Douglass became a Republican Party stalwart and "stumped" for the party in every post-bellum campaign until his death. Although he was no longer an outsider, Douglass did not give up the gadfly aspect of his former role. He now worked from *within* the party ranks to radicalize the Republican platform as described above. . . .

In order to rid America of slavery Lincoln needed "the earnest sympathy and the powerful cooperation of his loyal fellowcountrymen. Without this *primary* and *essential condition to success,* his efforts must have been in vain and utterly fruitless." (Emphasis added.) Douglass the agitator was free to stir up fierce passions, to anger his opponents. But Douglass the agitator knew that Lincoln the statesman did not have the same freedom. Douglass acknowledged that, "had [Lincoln] put the abolition of slavery before the salvation of the Union, he would have inevitably driven from him a powerful class of the American people and rendered resistance to rebellion impossible." Profound social change in a republic requires not only agitators and radicals of Douglass' ilk, but also statesmen of Lincoln's stature. The latter recognize, as Douglass pointed out, that as statesmen they *must* consult the country's sentiment. If they move too far ahead of it, they simply cannot attain success. Measured against genuine abolitionists, Lincoln had seemed "tardy, cold, dull, and indifferent." But measured against popular sentiment, "he was swift, zealous, radical and determined."

Lincoln's example taught Douglass the lesson of democratic statesmanship: the indispensability of popular support for the successful initiation of great social change. He continued to introduce moral principles into discussions of public affairs, but he did so and performed his role as agitator in the postwar years from within the Republican Party.

Douglass and Antislavery Violence

James H. Cook

In the excerpt from the following essay, James H. Cook, a former staff member of the Frederick Douglass Papers, examines Douglass's relationship with John Brown, a white, militant abolitionist. Brown sought in vain to draw Douglass into an abolitionist conspiracy to infiltrate the South in order to assist slaves in large-scale escape efforts. Brown's plotting culminated in an unsuccessful assault in October 1859 on the federal armory at Harpers Ferry in present-day West Virginia. Cook analyzes the interaction of intellectual, political, and psychological factors governing Douglass's evolving views toward the employment of violent antislavery tactics. In particular, Cook attempts to explain why Douglass so loudly praised Brown's willingness to sacrifice his life for the abolitionist cause while he personally adopted the physically safer role of antislavery propagandist.

The topic of Frederick Douglass's views on antislavery violence is hardly a novel one. Numerous scholars have delineated the evolution of Douglass's thinking on violence, but few have strictly tracked the level of violence within his personal life. None have taken on the sticky task of reconciling the two. This essay's main contention is that there existed an inverted relationship between the level of violence within Douglass's rhetoric and that which he experienced within his personal life. That is, as Douglass was drawn toward a more militant position on antislavery violence, he coincidentally experienced a decrease in the amount of violence he encountered in his day-to-day existence. Though the evidence suggests that this pattern was more circumstantial than by design, it nonetheless produced in Douglass a form

James H. Cook, "Fighting with Breath, Not Blows: Frederick Douglass and Antislavery Violence," *Antislavery Violence: Sectional, Racial, and Cultural Conflict in Antebellum America,* edited by John R. McKivigan and Stanley Harrold. Knoxville: The University of Tennessee Press, 1999. Copyright © 1999 by The University of Tennessee Press. Reproduced by permission.

of self-consciousness about the relationship between one's use of violence and the level of commitment to the anti-slavery cause.

This growing self-awareness owed much to Douglass's close relationship with John Brown. As a corollary to his spirited defense of Brown's activities in the 1850s, Douglass drew sharp distinctions among his fellow abolitionists. He praised those who, like Brown, were willing to spill blood (including their own) in the fight against slavery and derided those who were not. In so doing, Douglass ironically accentuated his own personal distance from antislavery violence. For any critics who perceived in his personal course of action a general inconsistency, however, Douglass felt nothing but disdain. . . .

JOHN BROWN'S INFLUENCE ON DOUGLASS

Though scholars within the past twenty years have sought to diminish the significance of Brown's influence upon Douglass, it is clear from the written record that Brown loomed large in Douglass's consciousness. At their initial meeting in 1847, Brown laid out his famous "Subterranean Pass Way" scheme, by which an armed band of freedom fighters would penetrate deep into the heart of slave territory via the Alleghany ridge, transforming slaves into soldiers along the way. Though Douglass was at first skeptical of Brown's methods, he noted in his 1881 autobiography that "from this night spent with John Brown, my utterances became more and more tinged by the color of this man's strong impressions." At the 1847 meeting, Brown advanced several key arguments, two of which Douglass gradually incorporated into his antislavery repertoire. One was that slavery constituted a "state of war," and that it "could only be destroyed by blood-shed." Another was that "no people . . . could have self-respect, or be respected, who would not fight for their freedom." Following Brown's lead, Douglass particularly cultivated the second point beginning in the early 1850s.

In January 1851, Brown formed the League of the Gileadites, a quasi-military organization of fifty-four African Americans set up exclusively to resist violently attempts to enforce the Fugitive Slave Law. While forming the league, Brown circulated a document he entitled "Words of Advice." Utilizing shame as a motivational device, he severely rebuked black Americans who would not stand up and fight for their rights, suggesting that white America would consider them human beings only if they physically resisted slavehunters and kidnappers. Brown's text represented not only an exhortation to his black compatriots, but a foreshadowing of his own fiery test of courage eight years into the future. "Nothing so charms the American people," he wrote, "as personal bravery. The trial for life of one bold and to some extent successful man, for defending his rights in good earnest, would arouse more sympathy throughout the nation than the accumulated wrongs and sufferings of more than three millions of our submissive colored population."

In the same week that Brown wrote these words, Douglass chastised New York African Americans for allowing a runaway slave, Henry Long, to be captured from their midst without offering any resistance. "Some explanation, some apology for the apparent indifference and utter inactivity manifested by the colored people of New York City, is demanded," he thundered to a Rochester audience. Eight months later, Douglass offered a critique even more plainly in line with Brown's. Rather than stressing collective guilt as a motivating factor, Douglass focused heavily upon the shame component. The "lamblike submission of blacks to the violation of their rights has only served to create contempt for them in the public mind," he wrote. "The black man could gain not only self-respect but also a measure of public dignity by fighting against his enslavers."

In 1854, Douglass had continued to expand upon the theme of African American resistance, both in the North and South, by posing the deceptively simple question, "Is it Right and Wise to Kill a Kidnapper?" Douglass concluded that the killing of those who attempt to "play the bloodhound" was "as innocent, in the sight of God, as would be the slaughter of a ravenous wolf in the act of throttling an infant." Three years later, after proclaiming the peaceful abolition of slavery to be an "almost hopeless" cause, Douglass levied nothing less than a death sentence upon slaveholders. "Terrible as it [slave insurrection] will be, we accept and hope for it," Douglass wrote; "The slaveholder has been tried and sentenced, his execution only waits the finish to the training of his executioners. He is training his own executioners." Douglass's choice of an execution as metaphor must have seemed more than a little careless to those who were familiar with his strict opposition to capital punishment throughout the same period. If anything, this contradiction revealed how uniquely heinous a crime Douglass considered slave-holding to have been.

OUT OF HARM'S WAY

As the Kansas conflict [between proslavery and antislavery factions] began to unfold in 1854, Douglass's personal removal from violent struggle against slavery and discrimination became all the more evident. While he continued vehemently to press others toward the front, he did so increasingly from a rearward position. In spite of numerous warning signs of approaching violence, Douglass did not hesitate to prod his fellow African Americans to go to Kansas in order to serve as a buffer against slavery's advance. Douglass at first tried to convince black Americans that the territory was secure from violent dangers. After declaring that "the coast is clear" and that they would experience little if any hindrance from their white neighbors, he then returned to shame and guilt themes. "Whether regarded from the point of the duty to the Slave . . . or from the point of duty to themselves," he emphatically enjoined, "*they ought to go* into that Territory as *permanent settlers.*"

While he made it abundantly clear that Kansas desperately needed black farmers, laborers, and families, Douglass apparently believed that it had filled its quota of black newspaper editors and lecturers. African Americans, both slave and free, continued throughout the decade to populate the territory in significant numbers, provoking intense hostility among white settlers. Despite their violent disagreements over slavery, proslavery and free soil whites in Kansas shared a common attitude toward this black population. In the same week that Douglass pronounced the territory conducive to black resettlement, an abolitionist on the scene, Samuel L. Adair, painted a different picture. Of the free soil forces, he wrote, "their free soil is free soil for white, but not for the black. They hate slavery, but they hate the negro worse. Their language is, 'if we must have niggers here, let them be slaves, not free.'"

As conditions deteriorated for blacks living on the plains, Douglass's presence could have exercised more than a little influence on what one observer referred to as "the large population of ignorance" there. At least one resident believed this to be the case when he wrote to a relative in the East, complaining that among free soilers "the great cry now is nigger, nigger, nigger," adding that he wished Douglass would "come here and lecture." As his speaking itinerary reveals, though, Douglass felt no need to travel through the territory in the crucial years prior to the Civil War. Douglass instead nudged others whom he considered more qualified, like his friend and supporter Gerrit Smith, toward the task of reforming Kansas society. "I am glad you gave three thousand dollars to the cause of freedom in Kansas," he wrote Smith in early 1856, "and hope you will use your power in that country to shame the free state men out of their contemptible selfishness in excluding the free colored men out of that territory." Douglass's main function in the Kansas conflict would be as defender of Brown's reputation in the East.

On May 22, 1856, in a speech delivered in Rochester, Douglass harshly condemned the murders of several Free State men, giving especial notice to the grisly death of Rees P. Brown (no relation to John Brown). Proslavery forces had attacked Brown, the leader of Leavenworth free-staters, hacking him to death with a hatchet and unceremoniously dumping his corpse on his wife's doorstep. This final indignity drew severe censure from Douglass. Yet, acts similar to those which Douglass termed "barbaric" to a Rochester audience on Thursday night were committed by John Brown and his sons two nights later on the Pottawatomie Creek. In what remains his most controversial action, Brown directed his sons to drag five men deemed to be proslavery from their homes in the middle of the night and hack them to death with broadswords. In a manner similar to his broad pronouncements regarding slave rebellion, Douglass suspended, in Brown's case, an otherwise vehement opposition to revenge-based justice. "He has been charged with murder!" he editorialized one month later. "What could be more absurd! If he has sinned in anything, it is in that he has spared lives of murderers, when he had the power to take vengeance upon them."

Like many observers at the time, Douglass was initially misinformed about the facts of the incident. His statement, on its face, is similar to those made by other prominent abolitionists in the wake of the massacre, many of whom considered the charges against Brown too fantastic to believe. But if Douglass held that Brown had not carried out the killings, he nevertheless clearly felt that Brown was remiss in not having done so. Indeed, he strongly hinted that Brown should have exacted revenge upon proslavery "murderers" whenever circumstances would allow. This was no broad, abstract endorsement of slave insurrections or the killing of slave hunters in the name of self-defense. It was rather a cold, blunt advocacy of what turned out to be, in fact, Brown's actual crime. Perhaps Douglass would not have been as enthusiastic about the supposed murders if he had known of their grisly details or that some of the victims' status as "proslavery men" was nebulous. This is unlikely, however, considering his future statements, penned well after the facts of the case became widely known. "The horrors wrought by his iron hand cannot be contemplated without a shudder," Douglass wrote of Brown in 1881, "but it is the shudder that one feels at the execution of a murderer. . . . To call out a murderer at midnight, and without note or warning, judge or jury, run him through with a sword, was a terrible remedy for a terrible malady."

THE HARPERS FERRY PLOT

After Brown's mission in Kansas came to a close, he returned to the East and embarked on several fundraising tours for his "Subterranean Pass Way" scheme. Whenever passing through Rochester, he stayed with Douglass and openly sought his counsel. The most spirited defense mustered by Douglass on Brown's behalf while the latter was still alive came in response to a decided lack of enthusiasm on the part of Douglass's neighbors toward Brown. When Brown failed to receive the grandiose reception to which Douglass believed he was entitled during an 1859 visit, Douglass unleashed a furious diatribe against the antislavery community. In so doing, however, he merely highlighted the ever-widening chasm separating his advocacy of violence from his personal involvement in it. Before leveling criticisms at Brown, Douglass righteously intoned, reformers and politicians should take a quick glance into the mirror. "Have they been sincere in what they have said of their love of freedom?" Douglass asked. "Have they really desired to head off, hem in, and dam up the desolating tide of slavery? If so, does it not seem that one who has suffered, and periled everything in accomplishing these very ends, has some claims upon their grateful respect and esteem?"

More to the point, Douglass insisted, was that Brown, unlike his contemporaries, was a man who did more than just give speeches. "Had John Brown been a man of words, rather than deeds," Douglass wrote, "had he been noted for opposing slavery with his breath, rather than with blows . . . his reception here would have been cordial, and perhaps enthusiastic. . . ." Not only were Brown's critics feeble and pusillanimous, but they always extended praise to the wrong people while withholding it from those who truly deserved it.

Then, employing a bit of overkill, Douglass suggested that individuals who criticized Brown could not be considered true abolitionists. Such criticism was insulting to a man like Brown "who will forsake home, family, ease, and security, and in the cause of liberty go forth to spill his blood, if need be. . . ." Most damning of all was Douglass's suggestion that abolitionists who could not match Brown's level of commitment were not legitimate, but were in fact agents of slavery. "The basis of [Brown's] idea of duty is comprehensive," Douglass lauded, "that a case of [slavery] is one which every human being is solemnly bound to interfere; and that he who has the power to do so, and fails to improve it, is involved in the guilt of the original crime."

The Harpers Ferry raid and John Brown's death lay seven months in the future, but Douglass had already commenced the canonization process. His statements indicate that he embraced the notion of a hierarchy of commitment among antislavery reformers. There was no doubt in Douglass's mind as to who occupied the lone seat atop the pyramid. A more difficult question to answer is the following: where did Douglass place himself within that hierarchy? . . .

DEFENDING JOHN BROWN

Ironically, Douglass's strident defense of Brown's reputation beginning in 1856, which eventually included publicly denigrating the sincerity and commitment of his fellow abolitionists, only served to highlight his own stark differences with Brown. If these differences were not already evident to Douglass, they must have become so during the several weeks in January and February of 1858 when Brown lived under his roof. Day in and out, Douglass watched and listened as Brown ceaselessly tinkered with his Subterranean scheme, formulated a provisional constitution by which his army would govern, and corresponded with family members and supporters.

Though Douglass later wrote that be became bored with Brown's scheming and dreaming during the latter's stay in Rochester, evidence indicates that he felt something closer

DOUGLASS'S LAST MEETING WITH JOHN BROWN

Writer Edward J. Renehan Jr. studied the conspiracy of abolitionists to support John Brown's intended attack on the Federal Arsenal at Harpers Ferry in order to capture arms for a massive slave uprising. In the following excerpt, Renehan describes the last attempt by Brown to recruit Douglass to join his raid into the South. Douglass brought a younger black, Shields Green, along to a clandestine rendezvous with Brown in southern Pennsylvania just days before the Harpers Ferry attack.

The place of meeting was an abandoned quarry near Chambersburg. Douglass remembered that he approached the old quarry "very cautiously, for John Brown was generally well armed, and regarded strangers with suspicion." The two men moved slowly around the edge of the lonesome, echoing place, the sound of their bootsteps bouncing eerily off the high rock walls. It seemed like a long time before they finally came upon the brooding figure of Brown seated on a ledge halfway up a chasm, a rifle across his legs. From here he had a good view to see whether Douglass had been followed. Slowly, Brown climbed down to greet his guests. "Come with me, Douglass," said Brown. "I want you for a special purpose. When I strike, the bees will begin to swarm, and I shall want you to help hive them." Douglass, however, stood by his previously voiced reservations about Brown's plan. Brown, Douglass was convinced, was doomed to both political and personal failure. Armed attack on the federal government would, argued Douglass, be a disaster. It would array the entire country against the abolition movement. His purpose in meeting Brown was not to allow himself to be recruited, but rather to try one last time to dissuade Brown from a course that would bode well for no one.

Douglass said Harpers Ferry was a "perfect steel-trap." "You will never get out alive," Douglass told Brown. Virginia would blow him and any hostages he might take sky-high, rather than he should hold Harpers Ferry one hour. Just as he had several months earlier, Brown shrugged off Douglass's doubts. Douglass left Brown in the quarry with his delusion of divinely assured success. He also left him with another soldier: Shields Green.

Edward J. Renehan Jr., *The Secret Six: The True Tale of the Men Who Conspired with John Brown.* New York: Crown Publishers, 1995.

to discomfort. In 1881, the year in which Douglass reflected extensively upon his relationship with Brown, both in his final autobiography and in a famous speech at Storer College in Harpers Ferry, an unknown admirer sent him a letter that had been written by Brown during his 1858 "residence" at the Douglass home. The momento sparked fresh memories of that crucial period when Douglass found himself increasingly distressed by Brown's arguments and plans. "He was a constant thorn in my side," Douglass wrote back to the admirer. "I could not help feeling that this man's zeal in the cause of my enslaved people was holier and higher than mine. . . . His call to me was 'Come up higher' and not being ready to rise to his height, his calls troubled me."

It is not surprising that the failed raid on Harpers Ferry, and especially Douglass's actions in relation to it, produced a crisis of conscience for Douglass, evoking his most candid views concerning his own personal commitment to antislavery violence. Several weeks before the planned attack, Brown met with Douglass at an abandoned stone quarry near Chambersburg, Pennsylvania. He attempted to enlist Douglass in his small army, hoping to utilize the black leader as a magnet for still more African American recruits. Realizing that the raid, as now formulated by Brown, had little chance of succeeding, Douglass decided against participating in the mission.

Due to his close association with Brown, Douglass scrambled to defend both his life and reputation following Brown's capture. Undoubtedly adding to any personal turmoil he might have felt at the time was raider John E. Cook's public accusation that Douglass had promised to lead reinforcements into Harpers Ferry, only to have backed out at the crucial moment. Writing from Canada three days after the raid, Douglass found himself in the unenviable position of denying any personal involvement in the raid while at the same time praising Brown's efforts. He quickly formulated what became a major theme in his standard characterizations of his relationship with Brown. "Mr. Cook may be perfectly right in denouncing me as a coward," he wrote. "I have always been more distinguished for running that fighting— and tried by the Harpers Ferry insurrection test, I am most miserably deficient in courage." Then, in what has become an oft-quoted passage, he added, "I am ever ready to write, speak, publish, organize, combine and even conspire against slavery when there is a reasonable hope of success. . . . 'The tools to those who can use them.' Let every man work for the abolition of slavery in his own way. I would help all and hinder none."

While the first statement was hardly novel, . . . the second represented a departure. Over the previous three years, Douglass had suggested that those who opposed Brown's methods were not true abolitionists. Only six months before the raid, he had told them in plain language that they were the minions of slavery. Now, in defending his own choices, Douglass tried to turn back the clock to a time when all abolitionists were equal in his sight. It was a sentiment that more than a few compatriots must have found disingenuous.

Douglass's statements after the raid suggest a defensive posture on his part, though he also made it abundantly clear that the only man whom he considered qualified to sit in judgment of him lay six feet in the ground at North Elba, New York. He brooked criticism from none other. In a highly revealing comment, made in his final autobiography, Douglass suggested that any opprobrium over his personal decisions prior to the raid came from a single source. "Some have thought that I ought to have gone with [Brown]," he wrote, "but I have no reproaches for myself at this point, and since I have been assailed only by colored men who kept even further from this brave and heroic man than I did, I shall not trouble myself much about their criticisms."

Douglass was likely referring to a few cursory swipes taken at him by black leaders immediately following the raid. The editors of the *Weekly Anglo-African* expressed disappointment when Douglass left the country, traveling first to Canada then to Britain. Such actions did not befit "a man of heroic mold" like Douglass, they suggested. J. Sella Martin hinted at cowardice when he scolded Douglass for "writing from the broad latitude of Canada West." Turning the tables on his critics, Douglass suggested that their own similar cowardice rendered any analysis of his actions, no matter how well intentioned, wholly inappropriate. His dismissal of black critics, in such a backhanded manner years after the fact, underscores Douglass's fierce unwillingness even to ponder the disconnections that some African Americans obviously had perceived between his words and actions.

Throughout the 1850s, Douglass pushed black Americans to resist physically against slaveholders and kidnappers. He urged them to pour into a decidedly hostile territory in order to serve as a buffer against the advance of slavery. He publicly expressed disappointment with those who abandoned the good fight for the "pure atmosphere" of Canada and Britain. He repeatedly nudged, cajoled, and goaded them into harm's way, and he insisted, if necessary, that they fight with their last breath against slavery. All this he did from what may be perceived as the comfort and security of a podium and editor's desk. Judging solely by the outcome of Brown's raid, the suggestion that Douglass "ought to have gone with Brown" seems foolhardy, callous, and even vicious. Viewed against a decade of Douglass's querulous demands of black Americans, however, the comment does not appear as outrageous. As he did with many parts of his public persona, Douglass carefully scripted and managed his mea culpas [apologies] regarding antislavery violence. Though forever willing to defer to the memory of Brown's moral authority, he refused to contemplate, let alone acknowledge, the feelings of other African American leaders on the matter. He maintained for the balance of his life an icy indifference to the opinions of black Americans regarding his abstention at Harpers Ferry. . . .

It is significant that the last recorded instance in which Frederick Douglass was involved in antislavery violence on a personal level took place on the one-year anniversary of John Brown's execution. With the secession crisis foremost in the public mind, a hostile crowd of Unionists and anti-abolitionists took control of a meeting at Boston's Tremont Temple at which Douglass was to have memorialized Brown. When the crowd tried to block his path to the podium, Douglass lowered his head "like a trained pugilist" and bulled his way through the throng. While the crowd rioted, Douglass defiantly continued to speak, exchanging barbs with hecklers, and even threatening to throttle one of them "in the manner of a slave-driver." When somebody grabbed away the chair on which he sat, Douglass grabbed it back and wrestled with several rowdies and a policeman before relinquishing it.

After the meeting reconvened at another location, Douglass unleashed a blistering diatribe against slaveholders, slave catchers, and the South in general. Much to the delight of the crowd—this one decidedly more antislavery than the first one—Douglass suggested that "the only way to make the

Fugitive Slave Law a dead letter, is to make a few dead slave-catchers. There is no need to kill them either—shoot them in the legs, and send them to the South living epistles of the free gospel preached here at the North (laughter and applause.)" For the first time in a decade, Douglass employed "real" violence against the proponents of slavery and racial discrimination. That it occurred as he attempted to present a eulogy on John Brown is perhaps more than coincidental. . . .

That the level of physical confrontation within Douglass's daily life declined at the very time that he turned to embrace the rhetoric of violence is an undeniable fact that invites critical analysis on some level. As a true intellectual, Douglass was forced into pondering this paradoxical arrangement and offering some form of self-explanation, if only in a quiet way, to the public. This impulse became particularly strong after Douglass launched a staunch defense of John Brown's mission in Kansas. Ultimately, the brave captain's radical activism and dramatic demise came to serve a dual, ironic purpose for Douglass, who by the late 1850s jealously guarded his position as the nation's leading black abolitionist.

First, it provided Douglass with the opportunity to resolve any misgivings or doubts that he may have felt over perceived inconsistencies between his words and actions. By canonizing Brown (even before his final, glorious mission), Douglass could continue to display solidarity with Brown even while placing his friend on a higher, more distant plane from the one he himself occupied. Second, and more important, Brown's ultimate sacrifice became the means by which Douglass deflected criticism levied against him by leading African Americans. It is this latter function that needs to be more fully examined. A great deal of insight into Douglass's peculiar brand of activism may be gained through a comparative study of his personal dealings with other black militant abolitionists, such as Henry Highland Garnet and Martin Delany, on the one hand, and with John Brown, on the other. Douglass's experiences with the former ranged from half-hearted cooperation, at best, to personal rivalry and political backbiting, at worst. Alternatively, Douglass professed absolute loyalty and admiration for Brown, a man with whom he seemingly shared so much, yet so little.

Douglass and Lincoln

Christopher N. Breiseth

Trained as an historian at Cornell University, Christopher N. Breiseth served for seventeen years as president of Wilkes University. In the essay excerpted below, Breiseth examines Frederick Douglass's relationship with Civil War-time president Abraham Lincoln. Breiseth finds that Douglass was disappointed with Lincoln's leadership early in that conflict because the president refused to make emancipation a Union war goal. Douglass's attitude began to change following Lincoln's issuance of the Emancipation Proclamation in September 1862. After that decree, Douglass met with the president three times to advise him and found his opinions received respectfully by Lincoln. By the war's end, Douglass had developed a faith in Lincoln's Republican Party as the guardian of black rights, which he would retain for the remainder of his life despite frequent disappointments.

The Civil War, whatever else it may have been, was America's struggle over slavery. The relationship between Frederick Douglass, born a slave in Maryland, and Abraham Lincoln, born in Kentucky to a poor white family, reveals much about the debate over race during the Civil War. The relationship between the two men was punctuated by profound disagreement but culminated in expressions of deep mutual regard. The evolution of their relationship closely paralleled the evolution of Lincoln's thoughts on race. As politician and President, Lincoln was masterful in conveying his earnest consideration of voices pressing in on him from every side. He heard the conflicting arguments of a nation at war with itself and sought to blunt the differences and establish a common ground for preserving the Union. Frederick Douglass, representing an almost powerless people, relentlessly bore in upon Lincoln the irresistible logic that the war could be won and the Union preserved only if slavery was abolished. Prov-

Christopher N. Breiseth, "Lincoln and Frederick Douglass: Another Debate," *Journal of the Illinois State Historical Society*, vol. 68, February 1975, pp. 9–13, 15–22, 25–26. Copyright © 1975 by the Illinois State Historical Society. Reproduced by permission.

ing the influence of one individual upon another is difficult and inconclusive. But one can say that by 1865 Lincoln and Douglass had a fundamental similarity of vision about the profound causes and consequences of the Civil War.

TWO SIMILAR MEN

In the volatile politics of the prewar decade, both Lincoln and Douglass displayed a combination of calm practicality and moral vigor: Lincoln helped build the Republican party by drawing together a coalition of widely differing groups and individuals who, though disagreeing on specific policies, understood the threat to the Union posed by the slavery issue. The groups Lincoln sought to mobilize included those at one extreme who opposed the extension of slavery into the territories, in part because they hated blacks and wished them confined to the South, and those abolitionists at the other extreme who regarded the enslavement of blacks as America's prime offense against mankind. If Lincoln was cautious in trying to build a Republican coalition, he was unequivocal in his judgment that slavery was morally wrong and that the nation could not continue to live half slave and half free. Helped by his rivalry with the defiant white supremacist Stephen A. Douglas, Lincoln acquired the political skills that conveyed to a troubled electorate a mixture of political common sense, honesty, and personal independence.

A remarkable personal independence also characterized Frederick Douglass. Brought into the abolitionist movement in the early 1840's by William Lloyd Garrison, Douglass was regarded as a prize exhibit of Negro manhood, but he gradually broke with the anti-political policies of Garrison and other white abolitionists. Douglass rejected the Garrisonian position that the Constitution was a proslavery document and that the free states should advocate secession from the morally reprehensible slave states. Douglass, through his own monthly journal, insisted upon the need to use the ballot and political parties to abolish slavery. Twenty years a slave, he could not separate abolitionist theories from the possible consequences of those theories for blacks still in slavery. His ideological caution extended to his own personal situation. In 1846 he had agreed to accept the help of English friends to buy his freedom from his old master, a concession to the slave system that many white abolitionists deplored. (Douglass reminded white critics that they did not have to worry that the Fugitive Slave Law might be enforced against them.) Douglass's practicality also led him to refuse to join John Brown's armed rebellion of slaves at Harpers Ferry. The decision was difficult because Douglass admired Brown above all others. But Douglass also understood that his best weapons in the cause of liberation were his tongue, his pen, and his disciplined intellect. Like Lincoln, a self-made man, Douglass was not prepared to weaken his hard-won position of leadership by actions that were out of harmony with his own character, temperament, and understanding of events.

DOUGLASS'S INITIAL OPINION OF LINCOLN

As he studied the situation in June, 1860, Douglass departed from many abolitionist colleagues and publicly applauded the nomination of Lincoln, whom he labeled a "radical republican . . . fully committed to the doctrine of the irrepressible conflict." During the campaign, however, as Lincoln opposed only the extension of slavery and did not advocate outright abolition, Douglass grew troubled. But, faced with the political realities of the election, he concluded that friends of abolition should not waste their votes on the Liberty party candidate. Douglass thought that Lincoln's election in November was a hopeful sign, but he feared that while Lincoln's guarantees to slaveowners during the campaign would preserve the Union they would actually prolong slavery. The situation looked so bleak that Douglass declared that the dissolution of the Union might be necessary for the cause of liberty. His own course, he told his readers in December, was clear. "We shall join in no cry, and unite in no demand less than the complete and universal *abolition* of the whole slave system. Slavery shall be destroyed."

The single objective of Lincoln's Inaugural Address, in the face of secession by several slave states, was to preserve the Union. Acknowledging that slavery was the only real source of disunion, Lincoln sought to reassure the southern states that he had no desire to interfere with their peculiar institution. He indicated support for the rights of free Negroes but guaranteed enforcement of the Fugitive Slave Law, and went so far as to state that he would not oppose a constitutional amendment permanently guaranteeing noninterference with the institution of slavery. Douglass was outraged. To grant the slaveholders the constitutional right of owning their slaves, he charged, was to give up the whole argument.

He found some solace in Lincoln's cautious interest in protecting the rights of free Negroes but was disgusted by the President's heartless attitude toward those still in slavery. . . .

THE IMPACT OF FORT SUMTER

The Rebels' attack on Fort Sumter in April, 1861, precipitating the outbreak of the Civil War, transformed Douglass's despair to hope. He thought that the attack would unite the efforts of the North to put down the rebellion and would inevitably strengthen the antislavery cause. "The slaveholders themselves have saved our cause from ruin!" Douglass exclaimed. Lincoln could end the war quickly, counseled Douglass, by calling blacks, slave and free, into a liberating army that would raise the banner of emancipation among slaves. In July, Douglass insisted that there should be no escaping the central fact of the war. "The very stomach of this rebellion is the Negro in the condition of the slave."

Lincoln did not take Douglass's advice. He refused to enlist free blacks as soldiers. He did not at first countermand the orders of generals who refused to give protection to slaves escaping into Union lines. He delayed authorizing General Benjamin Butler's practice of considering escaped slaves as contraband. . . . Finally, in August, he countermanded the emancipation proclamation of General John C. Frémont. By October, Douglass concluded that Lincoln's unfolding strategy had been determined by his desire to keep the border slave states in the Union, and those slave states, Douglass held, were a millstone about the neck of the government and served as a shield for the treason of the cotton states.

Towards the end of 1861 Lincoln seemed to Douglass to be moving in a more hopeful direction. By November, Lincoln had approved the confiscation of Rebel property, tacitly allowed protection for fugitive slaves behind Union lines, and authorized use by Union forces of black labor. But when Lincoln, in his annual message in December, proposed colonization of freedmen, Douglass privately confessed to his bewilderment at "the spectacle of moral blindness, infatuation and helpless imbecility which the Government of Lincoln presents."

In March, 1862, Lincoln asked for a joint resolution of Congress for compensated emancipation. Sounding more like Douglass and other abolitionists, Lincoln told Congress that to deprive the slave states of their hope to secure slavery permanently would substantially end the rebellion. In April, Lincoln signed the bill to emancipate slaves in the District of Columbia, a move that Douglass happily described as "the first great step toward the righteousness which exalts a nation.". . .

EMANCIPATION AS A WAR GOAL

Despite Lincoln's . . . ambivalence about emancipation, . . . on September 22, 1862, [he] issued his Preliminary Emancipation Proclamation, forever freeing, as of January 1, 1863, all slaves residing within a state or part of a state in rebellion. He had carefully been preparing the ground of public opinion for that controversial act.

The two great objectives, preservation of the Union and abolition of slavery, had now begun to come together. Douglass was jubilant. "Common sense, the necessities of war, to say nothing of the dictation of justice and humanity have at last prevailed," he wrote. "We shout for joy that we live to record this righteous decree." Douglass had no fear that the President would turn back: "If he has taught us to confide in nothing else, he has taught us to confide in his word." Despite some last-minute maneuvering to induce the slave states to lay down their arms and avoid outright emancipation, Lincoln was true to his word. The Emancipation Proclamation issued on January 1, 1863, made no mention of compensation or colonization. Moreover, blacks were at last allowed to put on the Union Army uniform. Many abolitionists charged that the proclamation only ended slavery where the Union had no power and left it untouched among loyal Union slaveholders, but Douglass responded with a 2,000-mile speechmaking tour in behalf of Lincoln's righteous act. "Assuming that our Government and people will sustain the President and his Proclamation," Douglass told a New York audience in February, "we can scarcely conceive of a more complete revolution in the position of a nation." It was time to stop fighting the Rebels with only the North's soft white hand, Douglass said, and to unleash its iron black hand. . . .

DOUGLASS THE MILITARY RECRUITER

In a broadside titled "Men of Color, To Arms!" printed in papers throughout the North, Douglass declared to his black brethren that he could at last counsel them to take up arms. But the hideous draft riots in New York City in July, 1863, in which blacks were beaten to death, and their homes, orphanages, and churches burned, provided ominous evidence of the depth of northern white prejudice. Black regiments (in which Douglass's own sons served) went into bloody battle amidst threats by Jefferson Davis to enslave or butcher black prisoners. Meanwhile, in almost every way the black troops were given inferior treatment by the Union Army. After six months of effort, Douglass surveyed the situation, and in August told Major George L. Stearns, who was in charge of black recruitment, that he could no longer urge black men to fight unless Lincoln promised them the same protection given white soldiers. . . .

Stearns persuaded Douglass to travel to Washington and lay his grievances before Lincoln. Douglass expected to wait half a day in the crowded White House anterooms on August 10, 1863. But within moments after announcing himself, he was summoned to see the President. . . .

The President received the former slave as a gentleman. Douglass urged Lincoln to pay black soldiers wages equal to those paid white soldiers; to protect black prisoners like any other soldiers; to retaliate in kind for any black prisoners killed in cold blood by the Confederates and, finally, to reward black soldiers by distinction and promotion precisely as whites were rewarded. Lincoln responded to Douglass's remarks by saying that prejudice against blacks could be overcome only gradually. Black soldiers, Lincoln said, should be willing to serve under any conditions because they had stronger motives for fighting than did the white troops. As for protection of black prisoners, the President declared that the recent bloody losses of blacks at Milliken's Bend, Port Hudson, and Fort Wagner were necessary to prepare the way for his "Order of Retaliation" of July 30. In time, Lincoln promised, black troops would receive equal treatment. He also promised to sign any commission for black soldiers recommended by the Secretary of War. For his part, Lincoln protested against a public charge by Douglass that Lincoln was slow and vacillating. Lincoln admitted that he might seem slow; but to the charge of being vacillating, he objected. "Mr. Douglass," Lincoln said. "I do not think that charge can be sustained; I think it cannot be shown that when I have once taken a position, I have ever retreated from it." In relating that remark to the annual meeting of the American Anti-Slavery Society in December 1863, Douglass described it as the most significant point in their conversation. Although not in total agreement with Lincoln's views, Douglass "was so well satisfied with the man and the educating tendency of the conflict" that he determined to continue recruiting black men for the Union cause.

After his interview with Lincoln, Douglass proceeded directly to Secretary of War Edwin M. Stanton and came away with what he regarded as the pledge of a commission and orders to join General Lorenzo Thomas as assistant adjutant in recruiting black troops in the Mississippi Valley. Douglass hurried home to Rochester, New York, and wrote his valedictory for *Douglass' Monthly*, ending a journal that, under various names, had been his mouthpiece for nearly sixteen years. But the commission never came, and Douglass refused the request to join Thomas. Douglass privately ascribed Stanton's reversal to timidity to face a step that suggested a policy of racial equality. He complained to Stearns that he considered himself "trifled with and deceived."

Douglass made nothing of the rebuff in public. In articles and speeches, he carried on his efforts to convert the Union cause into an unsparing war for the total abolition of slavery. . . .

WINNING BLACKS THE VOTE

As he looked towards the 1864 presidential election, Douglass regarded the key issue to be the enfranchisement of blacks in the South to assure a just peace. He attacked Lincoln bitterly for his silence on the issue. Unknown to Douglass, Lincoln had taken a modest step towards black suffrage. In March, 1864, he had suggested in a letter to Michael Hahn, governor of the Louisiana government set up under the amnesty proclamation of December, 1863, that the franchise be given to blacks who were very intelligent and who had fought gallantly for the Union. "They would probably help, in some trying time to come, to keep the jewel of liberty within the family of freedom," he said. Lincoln stressed that the proposal was only a suggestion, however, and added that the contents of the letter were confidential. John Eaton, a key figure in government efforts for the freedmen, was aware of Douglass's dissatisfaction and reported it to Lincoln in August. The President asked Eaton to arrange another interview and wondered if Douglass knew of the contents of the letter to Hahn. Lincoln had assured Eaton "that considering the conditions from which Douglass rose, and the position to which he had attained, he was, in his judgment, one of the most meritorious men in America."

The interview was arranged, and Douglass found Lincoln on August 19 in a melancholy mood. The Union forces seemed unable to turn back the Rebels, and cries for peace were heard everywhere. Lincoln feared that his own reelection was in doubt. His "To Whom It May Concern" letter, making abolition one of the conditions for peace, had caused a furor among some of his supporters. Lincoln brought out the draft of a letter that had been written to reassure his friends. In that letter Lincoln said that he could not carry on a war for abolition without the support of the country and the Congress. Douglass objected strongly to the letter. "It would be given a broader meaning than you intend to convey," Douglass explained. "It would be taken as a complete surrender of your anti-slavery policy, and do you serious damage. In answer to your Copperhead accusers, your friends can make the argument of your want of power, but you cannot wisely say a word on that point." Lincoln did not send the letter. Lincoln then asked Douglass to plan a kind of underground railroad to help slaves escape to the North before war's end. That plan was prompted by Lincoln's fear for the fate of slaves in Rebel states should he lose the election or be forced to conclude the war on terms short of complete abolition.

Douglass returned home and began making plans for the new underground railroad. Douglass told Eaton that he was satisfied that Lincoln was doing all that circumstances permitted. From that date Douglass's enthusiastic regard and support for Lincoln were apparent. Eaton wrote later that the encounter was an illustration of how Lincoln handled his critics, drawing them in to wrestle with problems as they looked from the presidential desk. The letter Lincoln showed Douglass and the proposal for an underground railroad may have been devices for enlisting Douglass's involvement in the fate of the Lincoln administration; the encounter also indicates that Lincoln treated Douglass with respect. Less than one month later the outlook for the Union cause had improved. Sherman's capture of Atlanta turned the tide of the war and assured Lincoln's reelection. . . .

Douglass did not campaign actively for Lincoln because, he said, the Republicans "did not wish to expose themselves to the charge of being the 'N—r' party." He did express his views to the Colored National Convention, which met in Syracuse,

New York, in the first week of October. In his "Address to the People of the United States," he sought to underscore the identity of interest between the freed black man and a unified, healthy United States. The address acknowledged Lincoln's antislavery sentiment but expressed alarm at the devious efforts of the Republican party to hide that sentiment.

Douglass attended the inaugural ceremony on March 4, 1865, and heard Lincoln make an unequivocal commitment to abolition. While the most often quoted portion of the speech is its last sentence, beginning, "With malice towards none, with charity for all," the section that most moved Douglass spelled out Lincoln's belief that Divine Providence intended slavery to be abolished. Transcending the cold, legalistic language of so many of his wartime utterances, including the Emancipation Proclamation, Lincoln declared:

> Fondly do we hope—fervently do we pray—that this mighty scourge of war may speedily pass away. Yet, if God wills that it continue, until all the wealth piled by the bond-man's two hundred and fifty years of unrequited toil shall be sunk, and until every drop of blood drawn with the lash, shall be paid by another drawn with the sword, as was said three thousand years ago, so still it must be said, "the judgments of the Lord, are true and righteous altogether."

After the address Douglass availed himself of the citizen's right to shake hands with the President at a White House reception in the East Room. In the receiving line Lincoln told Douglass he had seen him during the speech and asked how he liked it. Douglass hesitated, not wishing to detain the President. "No, no," Lincoln said, "you must stop a little, Douglass; there is no man in the country whose opinion I value more than yours. I want to know what you think of it." "Mr. Lincoln," Douglass replied, "that was a sacred effort." "I am glad you liked it!" Lincoln said. Douglass passed on, "feeling that any man, however distinguished, might well regard himself honored by such expressions from such a man." Douglass was perhaps uniquely qualified among all the people in Lincoln's acquaintance to comprehend and acknowledge the moral and political significance of Lincoln's ascribing to Divine intent the Civil War as the instrument for abolishing slavery. . . .

When news of the assassination reached Rochester, Frederick Douglass warned his fellow townspeople not to be in too much haste to restore the Union of North and South. "Let us not be in a hurry to clasp to our bosom the spirit that gave birth to Booth. . . . When we take . . . as brethren, our Southern foes, let us see to it that we take also our Southern friends. Let us not forget that justice to the Negro is safety to the nation."

Eleven years later, on April 14, 1876, Douglass delivered an address at the unveiling of the Freedmen's Memorial Monument to Lincoln. The speech was the black liberator's testament to the white emancipator, before an audience of common people and the nation's leaders, including President Grant. Lincoln was "preeminently the white man's President," Douglass explained, "ready and willing at any time during the first years of his administration to deny, postpone, and sacrifice the rights of humanity in the colored people to promote the welfare of the white people of this country." Black Americans, on the other hand, were his "step-children by adoption." For whites, Douglass declared, "Abraham Lincoln saved . . . a country, [but] he delivered us from a bondage, according to Jefferson, one hour of which was worse than ages of the oppression your fathers rose in rebellion to oppose." The black man's faith in Lincoln was often taxed and strained to the uttermost, but never failed. . . .

"Viewed from the genuine abolition ground," Douglass said, "Mr. Lincoln seemed tardy, cold, dull, and indifferent; but measuring him by the sentiment of his country, a sentiment he was bound as a statesman to consult, he was swift, zealous, radical, and determined."

Abraham Lincoln fought for the Union. Douglass fought for the abolition of slavery. Each viewed the other's issue in light of his own. The men and the issues came together at the climax of a Civil War that saved the Union and abolished slavery. Douglass was the spokesman for nearly 180,000 black men whose fighting Lincoln regarded as decisive in saving the Union. Lincoln came to understand their struggle for freedom and his role as an instrument of their emancipation. From Douglass's perspective, Lincoln at last grasped the enormity of African chattel slavery, seeing it as destructive of the founding principles of the Republic as well as of the humanity of black Americans. Lincoln's teachers, we may surmise, included hard, irrepressible circumstances and men like Frederick Douglass who insisted that the equalitarian assumptions of the Declaration of Independence and the Constitution were at the heart of the struggle against the slaveholders. The figure of Frederick Douglass personified the insistent voice of black Americans.

CHAPTER 3

DOUGLASS AS A CIVIL RIGHTS LEADER

PEOPLE
WHO MADE
HISTORY

FREDERICK DOUGLASS

Preserving the Abolitionist Conception of the Civil War

David W. Blight

David W. Blight became interested in Frederick Douglass as a graduate student at the University of Wisconsin in the 1980s. His research culminated in the award-winning book *Frederick Douglass's Civil War: Keeping Faith in Jubilee* (1989). Today, Blight is chair of the history department at Amherst College in Massachusetts and recently published *Race and Union: The Civil War in American Memory*, which explores how the United States achieved sectional harmony after the Civil War by ignoring the role of slavery and race in causing that conflict while celebrating the common valor of white Union and Confederate soldiers. In the article excerpted below, Blight explores this same theme and demonstrates that Douglass eloquently criticized his contemporaries who forget the high moral purpose of the Union cause in their desire to conciliate white Southern feelings.

In the first week of January 1883, on the twentieth anniversary of the Emancipation Proclamation, a distinguished group of black leaders held a banquet in Washington, D.C., to honor the nineteenth century's most prominent Afro-American intellectual, Frederick Douglass. The banquet was an act of veneration for Douglass, an acknowledgment of the aging abolitionist's indispensable role in the Civil War era, a ritual of collective celebration, and an opportunity to forge historical memory and transmit it across generations. . . .

In his formal remarks at the banquet, Douglass demonstrated that during the last third of his life (he lived from 1818

David W. Blight, "'For Something Beyond the Battlefield': Frederick Douglass and the Struggle for the Memory of the Civil War," *Journal of American History*, vol. 75, March 1989, pp. 1,156, 1,158–62, 1,173–78. Copyright © 1989 by the *Journal of American History*. Reproduced by permission.

until 1895), a distinguishing feature of his leadership was his quest to preserve the memory of the Civil War as he believed blacks and the nation should remember it. Douglass viewed emancipation as the central reference point of black history. Likewise the nation, in his judgment, had no greater turning point, nor a better demonstration of national purpose. On the twentieth anniversary, Douglass sought to infuse emancipation and the war with the sacred and mythic qualities that he had always attributed to them. "This high festival . . . ," Douglass declared, "is coupled with a day which we do well to hold in sacred and everlasting honor, a day memorable alike in the history of the nation and in the life of an emancipated people." Emancipation day, he believed, ought to be a national celebration in which all blacks—the low and the mighty—could claim a new and secure social identity. But it was also an "epoch" full of lessons about the meaning of historical memory. "Reflection upon it (emancipation) opens to us a vast wilderness of thought and feeling," Douglass asserted. "Man is said to be an animal looking before and after. To him alone is given the prophetic vision, enabling him to discern the outline of his future through the mists of the past." Douglass challenged his fellow black leaders to remember the Civil War with awe. "The day we celebrate," he said, "affords us an eminence from which we may in a measure survey both the past and the future. It is one of those days which may well count for a thousand years.". . .

CIVIL RIGHTS IN RETREAT

Douglass's effort to forge memory into action that could somehow save the legacy of the Civil War for blacks—freedom, citizenship, suffrage, and dignity—came at a time when the nation appeared indifferent or hostile to that legacy. The richly symbolic emancipation day banquet of 1883 occurred only months before the United States Supreme Court struck down the Civil Rights Act of 1875, sacrificing the Civil War amendments, as the dissenting Justice John Marshall Harlan put it, and opening the door for the eventual triumph of Jim Crow laws across the South. The ruling in *United States v. Stanley,* better known as the *Civil Rights Cases,* declared that the equal protection clause of the Fourteenth Amendment applied only to states; a person wronged by racial discrimination, therefore, could look for redress only from state laws and courts. In effect, the decision would also mean that the discriminatory acts of private persons were beyond the safe-guards of the Fourteenth Amendment. . . .

Douglass interpreted the *Civil Rights Cases* as a failure of historical memory and national commitment. Reflecting on the Supreme Court decision in his final autobiography, Douglass contended that "the future historian will turn to the year 1883 to find the most flagrant example of this national deterioration." White racism, among individuals and in national policy, he remarked, seemed to increase in proportion to the "increasing distance from the time of the war." Douglass blamed not only the "fading and defacing effects of time," but more important, the spirit of reconciliation between North and South. Justice and liberty for blacks, he maintained, had lost ground from "the hour that the loyal North . . . began to shake hands over the bloody chasm." Thus, Douglass saw the Supreme Court decision as part of a disturbing pattern of historical change. Historical memory, he had come to realize, was not merely an entity altered by the passage of time; it was the prize in a struggle between rival versions of the past, a question of will, of power, of persuasion. The historical memory of any transforming or controversial event emerges from cultural and political competition, from the choice to confront the past and to debate and manipulate its meaning.

DOUGLASS'S USE OF HISTORY

Ever since the war Douglass had exhibited an increasingly keen sense of history. "I am this summer endeavoring to make myself a little more familiar with history," Douglass wrote to Gerrit Smith in 1868. "My ignorance of the past has long been a trouble to me." From the early days of Reconstruction, but especially by the 1870s, Douglass seemed acutely aware that the postwar era might ultimately be controlled by those who could best shape interpretations of the war itself. Winning the peace would not only be a matter of power, but also a struggle of moral will and historical consciousness. In the successful rise of the Democratic party, Douglass saw evidence that the South was beginning to win that struggle. In 1870 he complained that the American people were "destitute of political memory." But as he tried to reach out to both black and white readers with his newspaper, Douglass demanded that they not allow the country to "bury dead issues," as the Democrats wished. "The people cannot and will not forget the issues of the rebellion," Douglass admonished. "The Democratic party must continue to face the music of the past as well as of the present."

Some of Douglass's critics accused him of living in the past. American politics, declared a Liberal Republican newspaper in 1872, would "leave Mr. Douglass behind . . . vociferating the old platitudes as though the world had stopped eight years ago." To such criticisms Douglass always had a ready answer: he would *not forgive* the South and he would *never forget* the meaning of the war. At the Tomb of the Unknown Soldier in Arlington National Cemetery in 1871, on one of the first observances of Memorial Day, Douglass declared where he stood.

> We are sometimes asked in the name of patriotism to forget the merits of this fearful struggle, and to remember with equal admiration those who struck at the nation's life, and those who struck to save it—those who fought for slavery and those who fought for liberty and justice. I am no minister of malice . . . I would not repel the repentant, but . . . may my tongue cleave to the roof of my mouth if I forget the difference between the parties to that . . . bloody conflict . . . I may say if this war is to be forgotten, I ask in the name of all things sacred what shall men remember?

Douglass often referred to the preservation of the Union in glowing, nationalistic tones. But in the last third of his life, he demonstrated that the Civil War had also left many bitter elements of memory. Around the pledge to "never forget," Douglass organized his entire postwar effort to shape and preserve the legacy of the Civil War.

By intellectual predilection and by experience, Douglass was deeply conscious that history mattered. As the author of three autobiographies by the 1880s, he had cultivated deep furrows into his own memory. In a real sense, the Frederick Douglass who endures as an unending subject of literary and historical inquiry—because of the autobiographies—is and was the creature of memory. Moreover, Douglass deeply understood that peoples and nations are shaped and defined by history. He knew that history was a primary source of identity, meaning, and motivation. He seemed acutely aware that history was both burden and inspiration, something to be cherished and overcome. Douglass also understood that winning battles over policy or justice in the present often required an effective use of the past. He came to a realization that in late nineteenth-century America, blacks had a special need for a usable past. "It is not well to forget the past," Douglass warned in an 1884 speech. "Memory was given to man for some wise purpose. The past is . . . the mirror in which we may discern the dim outlines of the future and by which we may make them more symmetrical."

To all who look to history for meaning, those premises may seem obvious. But in the 1880s, according to Douglass, blacks occupied a special place in America's historical memory, as participants and as custodians. He understood his people's psychological need not to dwell on the horrors of slavery. But the slave experience was so immediate and unforgettable, Douglass believed, because it was a history

The Emancipation monument in Washington, D.C. Douglass stressed that the greatest achievement of the Civil War was emancipation.

that could "be traced like that of a wounded man through a crowd by the blood." Douglass urged his fellow blacks to keep *their* history before the consciousness of American society; if necessary, they should serve as a national conscience. "Well the nation may forget," Douglass said in 1888, "it may shut its eyes to the past, and frown upon any who may do otherwise, but the colored people of this country are bound to keep the past in lively memory till justice shall be done them." But as Douglass learned, such historical consciousness was as out of date in Gilded Age America as the racial justice he demanded.

In his retrospective thought about the Civil War, Douglass's intention was to forge enduring historical myths that could help win battles in the present. The deepest cultural myths—ideas and stories drawn from history that, through symbolic power, transcend generations—are the mechanisms of historical memory. Such myths are born of divergent experiences and provide the cultural weapons with which rival memories contest for hegemony. Douglass hoped that Union victory, black emancipation, and the Civil War amendments would be so deeply rooted in recent American experience, so central to any conception of national regeneration, so necessary to the postwar society that they would become sacred values, ritualized in memory. . . . Douglass's hope that emancipation could attain such indelible mythic quality was rooted in his enduring faith in the doctrine of progress and in his moral determinism, a belief that in a society of egalitarian laws good will outweigh evil in the collective action of human beings. Repeatedly, Douglass criticized the claim that emancipation came only by "military necessity" during the war. "The war for the Union came only to execute the moral and humane judgment of the nation," he asserted in 1883. "It was an instrument of a higher power than itself." What drew northerners to Memorial Day observances, Douglass maintained in 1878, was the "moral character of the war . . . the far-reaching . . . eternal principles in dispute, and for which our sons and brothers encountered . . . danger and death." By continuing to stress that sacred and ideological legacy of the war, Douglass exposed both his deepest sense of the meaning of the conflict and his fear that such meaning would not successfully compete with rival memories (in both North and South) and could, therefore, be lost. . . .

ABOLITIONIST MEMORY OF THE CIVIL WAR

The debate over the meaning of the war was not merely a question of remembering or forgetting. Douglass worried about historical amnesia because his version of the war, his memory, faltered next to the rival memories that resonated more deeply with the white majority in both North and South. Douglass may never have fully appreciated the complexity of the experience of the Civil War and Reconstruction for whites. The overwhelming number of white northerners who voted against black suffrage shared a bond of white supremacy with southerners who rejected the racial egalitarianism of Radical Reconstruction. The thousands of white Union veterans who remembered the war as a transforming personal experience, but not as the crucible of emancipation for four million slaves, had much in common with white Georgians who had found themselves in the path of Gen. William T. Sherman's [destructive] march to the sea. There were many rival memories of the war and its aftermath, and there was much need for forgetting and healing. . . . Douglass focused his efforts on the dangers of collective forgetting, not on its personal or cultural necessity. Douglass knew that his people, confined to minority status and living at the margins of society, could rarely afford the luxury of forgetting. Although he may not have thoroughly discriminated between the rival memories he confronted, he became fully aware of their power and their threat. Thus, with ever fewer sympathetic listeners by the late 1880s, Douglass was left with his lament that "slavery has always had a better memory than freedom, and was always a better hater."

Those were not merely words of nostalgic yearning for a vanished past uttered by a man out of touch with changing times. In a sense, Douglass was living in the past during the last part of his life; for him, the Civil War and Reconstruction were the reference points for the black experience in the nineteenth century. All questions of meaning, of a sense of place, of a sense of future for blacks in America drew upon the era of emancipation. . . . As an intellectual, Douglass had grown up with the abolition movement, the war, and its historical transformations. His career and his very personality had been shaped by those events. So, quite literally, Douglass's effort to preserve the memory of the Civil War was a quest to save the freedom of his people and the meaning of his own life.

Douglass embraced his role in preserving an abolitionist memory of the war with a sense of moral duty. In an 1883 speech in his old hometown of Rochester, New York, he was emphatic on that point.

> You will already have perceived that I am not of that school of thinkers which teaches us to let bygones be bygones; to let the dead past bury its dead. In my view there are no bygones in the world, and the past is not dead and cannot die. The evil as well as the good that men do lives after them. . . . The duty of keeping in memory the great deeds of the past, and of transmitting the same from generation to generation is implied in the mental and moral constitution of man.

But what of a society that did not widely share the same sense of history and preferred a different version of the past? Douglass's answer was to resist the Lost Cause by arguing for an opposite and, he hoped, deeper cultural myth—the abolitionist conception of the Civil War, black emancipation as the source of national regeneration.

In trying to forge an alternative to the Lost Cause, Douglass drew on America's reform tradition and constantly appealed to the Constitution and to the rule of law. Moreover, reversing a central tenet of the Lost Cause—the memory of defeat—Douglass emphasized the memory of victory, the sacrifices of the Union dead, and the historical progress he believed inherent in emancipation. This is what Douglass meant in an 1878 Memorial Day speech in Madison Square in New York, when he declared that "there was a right side and a wrong side in the late war which no sentiment ought to cause us to forget." . . .

He did sometimes imbue Union victory with an air of righteousness that skewed the facts. His insistence on the "moral" character of the war often neglected the complex, reluctant manner in which emancipation became the goal of the Union war effort. In structuring historical memory, Douglass could be as selective as his Lost Cause adversaries. His persistent defense of the Republican party after Reconstruction caused him to walk a thin line of hypocrisy. Indeed, Douglass's millennialist interpretation of the war forever caused him to see the conflict as a cleansing tragedy, wherein the nation had been redeemed of its evil by lasting grace. Douglass knew that black freedom had emerged *from* history more than from policy deliberately created by human agents. Moreover, he knew that emancipation had resulted largely from slaves' own massive self-liberation. But winning the battle over the legacy of the Civil War, Douglass knew, demanded deep cultural myths that would resonate widely in society. He knew that the struggle over memory was always, in part, a debate over the present. In his view, emancipation and black equality under law were the great results of the war. Hence, while urging old abolitionists not to give up their labors in 1875, Douglass contended that "every effort should now be made to save the result of this stupendous moral and physical contest." Moreover, nine years later Douglass warned that unless an abolitionist conception of the war were steadfastly preserved, America would "thus lose to after coming generations a vast motive power and inspiration to high and virtuous endeavor." Douglass labored to shape the memory of the Civil War, then, as a skillful propagandist, as a black leader confident of the virtue of his cause, and as an individual determined to protect his own identity. . . .

DOUGLASS REMAINS OPTIMISTIC

Although his jeremiads against the Lost Cause myth and his efforts to preserve an abolitionist memory of the conflict took on a strained quality, Douglass never lost hope in the regenerative meaning of the Civil War. It was such a great divide, such a compelling reference point, that the nation would, in time, have to face its meaning and consequences. In an 1884 speech, Douglass drew hope from a biblical metaphor of death and rebirth—the story of Jesus' raising Lazarus from the dead. "The assumption that the cause of the Negro is a dead issue," Douglass declared, "is an utter delusion. For the moment he may be buried under the dust and rubbish of endless discussion concerning civil service, tariff and free trade, labor and capital . . . but our Lazarus is not dead. He only sleeps."

Douglass's use of such a metaphor was perhaps a recognition of temporary defeat in the struggle for the memory of the Civil War. But it also represented his belief that, though the struggle would outlast his own life, it could still be won. Douglass gave one of his last public addresses on the final Memorial Day of his life (May 1894) at Mount Hope Cemetery in Rochester, were he would himself be buried some nine months later. The seventy-six-year-old orator angrily disavowed the sectional reconciliation that had swept the country. He feared that Decoration Day would become an event merely of "anachronisms, empty forms and superstitions." One wonders if the largely white audience in Rochester on that pleasant spring afternoon thought of Douglass himself as somewhat of an anachronism. In a country reeling from an economic depression in 1893, worried by massive immigration, the farmers' revolt, and the disorder of growing cities, Douglass's listeners (even in his old hometown) may not have looked beyond the symbolic trappings of the occasion. One wonders how willing they were to cultivate their thirty-year-old memory of the war and all its sacrifice, to face the deeper meanings Douglass demanded. The aged Douglass could still soar to oratorical heights on such occasions. He asked his audience to reflect with him about their "common memory." "I seem even now to hear and feel the effects of the sights and the sounds of that dreadful period," Douglass said. "I see the flags from the windows and housetops fluttering in the breeze. I see and hear the steady tramp of armed men in blue uniforms. . . . I see the recruiting sergeant with drum and fife . . . calling for men, young men and strong, to go to the front and fill up the gaps made by rebel powder and pestilence. I hear the piercing sound of trumpets." These were more than Whitmanesque pictures of bygone peril and glory. In a nation that now acquiesced in the frequent lynching of his people, that shattered their hopes with disfranchisement and segregation, Douglass appealed to history, to what for him was authentic experience, to the recognition scenes that formed personal and national identity. On an ideological level, where Douglass did his best work, he was still fighting the war. By 1894 he was as harsh as ever in his refusal to concede the Confederate dead any equal place in Memorial Day celebrations. "Death has no power to change moral qualities," he argued. "What was bad before the war, and during the war, has not been made good since the war." A tone of desperation entered Douglass's language toward the end of his speech. Again and again he pleaded with his audience not to believe the arguments of the Lost Cause advocates, however alluring their "disguises" might seem. He insisted that slavery had caused the war, that Americans should never forget that the South fought "to bind with chains millions of the human race."

No amount of nationalism, individualism, or compassion could ever change Douglass's conception of the memory and meaning of the Civil War. His pledge to "never forget" was both a personal and a partisan act. It was an assertion of the power of memory to inform, to inspire, and to compel action. Douglass was one of those nineteenth-century thinkers who by education, by temperament, and especially by experience believed that history was something living and useful. Even in the twilight of his life, there was no greater voice for the old shibboleth that the Civil War had been a struggle for union *and* liberty. "Whatever else I may forget," Douglass told those assembled at Mount Hope Cemetery, "I shall never forget the difference between those who fought for liberty and those who fought for slavery; between those who fought to save the Republic and those who fought to destroy it." The jubilee of black freedom in America had been achieved by heroic action, through forces in history, through a tragic war, and by faith. Among Douglass's final public acts, therefore, was to fight—using the power of language and historical imagination—to preserve that jubilee in memory and in reality. In a Rochester cemetery, he stood with the Union dead, waved the last bloody shirts of a former slave, a black leader, and a Yankee partisan, and anticipated the dulling effects of time and the poet Robert Lowell's vision of "the stone statues of the abstract Union soldier" adorning New England town greens, where "they doze over muskets and muse through their sideburns."

A Composite American Nationality

Waldo E. Martin Jr.

In 1882 Douglass's first wife Anna Murray Douglass died. Only seventeen months later, Douglass surprised his own children and angered many long-term black admirers by marrying the forty-six-year-old Helen Pitts, his white former clerk at the Recorder of Deeds office in the District of Columbia. Historian Waldo E. Martin Jr., now professor of history at the University of California-Berkeley, in the following selection from his 1984 intellectual biography of Douglass, examines Douglass's views on race and miscegenation. Martin concludes that Douglass's marriage to Pitts was consistent with his long-held belief that the United States would eventually conquer its racial divisiveness when its component races blended together literally, as well as culturally, into a "composite nationality."

Race was an ambiguous, albeit vital, concept in the nineteenth-century Western world. Among other things, it commonly referred to a nationality, a nation-state, an ethnologically distinct people, or simply an exotic and mysterious people. From individual personality to international relations, much of what was important to nineteenth-century Western civilization was understood in the context of race. What environment had been to the preceding century—especially to the enlightened humanist—race, to a large extent, became in the nineteenth century—especially to the romantic nationalist. Race came to function as a necessary, if not wholly sufficient, explanation for almost everything, including Western colonialism and imperialism. Dr. Robert Knox, influential British professor of anatomy, propounded this increasingly popular and powerful outlook. "Race," he wrote,

Waldo E. Martin Jr., *The Mind of Frederick Douglass*. Chapel Hill: The University of North Carolina Press, 1984. Copyright © 1984 by The University of North Carolina Press. Reproduced by permission.

"is everything: literature, science, art—in a word, civilization depends on it."

Racial thought before and throughout the nineteenth century revealed a complex and sometimes bewildering range of beliefs, attitudes, and ideals, ranging from benign paternalism to vicious racism. During the nineteenth century, however, the study of race assumed a theoretical and scientific mantle of sophistication as scientists, intellectuals, and propagandists endeavored to comprehend it by minimizing its characteristic ambiguity. Their failure illustrates the disastrous human impact of a potent human myth—race—and the invidious ramifications of its most malignant extreme—racism.

Race in nineteenth-century America clarified the status quo among the various known peoples and underlaid America's national identity. An acute awareness of racial differences was a critical factor enabling architects of the emerging United States to develop a sense of their own separate racial (Anglo) and national (American) identities which they fused into a single identity—Anglo-American. . . .

The representative American was white; the nonwhite was interloper who helped define an American through negative example. Not surprisingly, therefore, many influential whites attributed the cultural genius and historic promise of America to its Anglo-Saxon or Teutonic origins.

Each race, nevertheless, possessed its distinctive gifts. Racial heredity, rather than environment, signified the key to human history. For whites who had mastered their environment and achieved historical greatness, the process of continuing racial evolution permitted them to manipulate even further their environment and, thus, to affect the course of their future. For nonwhites still captive to their environment and basically barbarous, the permanently arrested process of racial evolution left them in an ominous state. Extinction appeared possible; genocide seemed reasonable. There was also an alleged "instinctive antipathy among the races." Nation building, as a result, necessitated racial purity; miscegenation was unnatural; and mulattoes were congenitally weak, immoral, and torn by "confused race instincts."

DOUGLASS REBUTS RACISM

The contemporary ascendency of racism seriously undermined the challenge to this racial orthodoxy. Those like

Frederick Douglass who struggled valiantly against that orthodoxy swam against the tide. Douglass, for instance, believed in both racial equality and cultural hierarchy. Although he agreed that each race had its special gifts, he believed human moral and mental endowments to be a function of environment and, consequently, alterable. More so than race and heredity, environment signified the key to history and culture. He saw no "instinctive antipathy among the races." Racial homogeneity and purity, therefore, were unnecessary for and detrimental to nation building; miscegenation was natural; and mulattoes were congenitally strong, moral, and racially well adjusted.

Indeed, human diversity undergirded human unity and equality in Douglass's world view. Paradoxically, he also believed in the romantic notion of peculiar racial gifts. His interpretation of these gifts reflected the common belief that each race had a unique genius and, as a result, a particular contribution to make to a comprehensive, though hierarchical, view of human culture and history. He shared, for example, the common nineteenth-century American belief in and admiration for a reputed Anglo-Saxon genius for republican democracy.

Douglass's belief in both the romantic concept of peculiar racial gifts and the Enlightenment concept of a singular human nature distinctly betrayed both the eclecticism of his thought and its often complex character. While praising Anglo-Saxons for republican democracy, he upbraided them for power madness and its evil consequences. "The love of power," he contended, "is one of the strongest traits of the Anglo-Saxon race." Furthermore, this "love of power and dominion, strengthened by two centuries of irresponsible power" buttressed slavery and racism. Intellectually, Douglass struggled ingeniously, yet unsuccessfully, to resolve his ambivalence toward Anglo-Saxons and races generally as well as the paradox of peculiar racial gifts amid human unity and equality. The dynamic mechanism of his approach toward both goals was a provocative version of the "melting-pot" theme—a composite American nationality. . . .

Douglass's ideal nation-state, society, and culture would have been raceless. Even if different races had coexisted in this utopia, it would have been raceless in the sense that race would not have been an issue. In reality, however, race rather than racelessness was omnipresent and determinative. Theoretically, race, like religion and national origin, could be partially overcome through assimilation. Still, the process of assimilation was not a panacea for the American dilemma of race, Douglass maintained. He consistently reiterated, regardless, his strong commitment to assimilation as a key factor in a possible solution. "There is but one destiny, it seems to me, left for us," he reminded his people in 1883, "and that is to make ourselves and be made by others a part of the American people in every sense of the word." He concluded, therefore, that "assimilation and not isolation is our true policy and our natural destiny. Unification for us is life; separation is death." Assimilation, unfortunately, meant cultural absorption into a white America: an implicit cultural rejection of a black America.

Besides its Anglo-American cultural framework, Douglass's assimilationism was thoroughly integrationist. He rejected Negro separatism, Negro colonization outside and within the continental United States, African repatriation schemes, and social and institutional segregation. Separate black institutions and communities he viewed as necessary but temporary expedients; a black means toward a humanist, yet culturally Anglo-American, end. . . .

ADVOCATE OF ASSIMILATION

The most controversial and revealing aspect of Douglass's assimilationism was his belief in miscegenation. He prophesied in 1886 that in the future the Negro "will be absorbed, assimilated, and will only appear finally, as the Phoenicians now appear . . . , in the features of a blended race." The primary evidence for this provocative forecast was the increasing number of mulattoes in the general population. He observed that "two hundred years ago there were two distinct and separate streams of human life running through this country. They stood at opposite extremes of ethnological classification: all black on the one side, all white on the other. Now, between these two extremes, an intermediate race has arisen, which is neither white nor black, neither Caucasian nor Ethiopian, and this intermediate race is constantly increasing."

Noting in another context that miscegenation had begun under Negro slavery, he proposed that now under the more propitious circumstances of Negro freedom, it would naturally increase. Full of hope and idealism, he argued that increasing miscegenation signified that "the tendency of the age is unification, not isolation; not to clans and classes; but to human brotherhood." Perhaps. The reality of racial strife, however, contradicted this interpretation.

Miscegenation inevitably evoked the specter of interracial marriage. Both represented a radical departure from the taboo against intimate contact between the races. Douglass's own interracial marriage attested to the depth of his commitment to miscegenation. In an ironic and misleading explanation, especially in light of his interracial marriage, he once contended that he neither advocated nor opposed interracial marriage and miscegenation. This alleged neutrality was an unsuccessful attempt to avoid identification with the advocacy of two social heresies that offended black race pride in addition to white racism. Douglass's unavoidable association with these social heresies lent credence among many to the criticism that his race pride was suspect.

Consistent with his egalitarian humanism, Douglass believed that assimilation, miscegenation, and interracial marriage constituted progressive developments. The hysterical American opposition to them, therefore, he construed as illogical and unfounded. Given his vision of the inevitability of full racial assimilationism in conjunction with America's rational bent, he believed that this bitter American prejudice against racial assimilationism would ultimately be overcome. Americans, he maintained, "easily adapt themselves to inevitable conditions, and all their tendency is to progress, enlightenment, and to the universal." In particular, black opposition to racial assimilationism, he maintained, reflected "the merest affectation and will never form an impassable barrier to the union of the two varieties." Nevertheless, the forces of progress, enlightenment, and universalism paradoxically left rational America's racial irrationality fundamentally intact. Once again, Douglass's utopian vision obscured the serious dislocation of his own age. . . .

A COMPOSITE RACIAL IDENTITY

The centerpiece of Douglass's grandiose racially assimilationist vision was his conceptualization of the United States as a composite nationality: "or cosmopolitan nation, the grandest and most comprehensive illustration of the human race." By blurring the distinction between the ideal and the reality of a composite nationality, he tried to enhance its viability while downplaying its utopian character. A racially diverse country like the United States, Douglass believed, necessitated a composite or mixed national identity. Rejecting the racist present, Douglass argued that the challenge to the future remained clear, though very difficult. "Can the white and colored people of this country," he asked, "be blended into a common nationality, and enjoy together, in the same country, under the same flag, the inestimable blessings of life, liberty, and the pursuit of happiness, as neighborly citizens of a common country?" His response, in spite of significant countervailing evidence, was yes. . . .

A composite American nationality exemplified in Douglass's mind an advance in sociocultural as well as biological evolution. As the mulatto represented the best of two races, a composite nationality represented the best in sociocultural and political relations. Douglass suggested that the marginal mulatto symbolized not only, paradoxically, a biological advance, but also the incongruence between race and a composite American nationality. Given that four-fifths of the world's people were nonwhite and the fact of America's racial diversity, a composite American nationality was an ethical as well as ethnological issue. Indeed, for Douglas, the evolution toward a composite nationality constituted more of a moral issue than an ethnological one; it was a matter of the unavoidable triumph of right as against the temporary and illusory triumph of race. . . .

BLENDING CULTURES TOGETHER

The process of Americanization, according to Douglass, compelled the various racial components of America "to lose, in a common character, all traces of their former distinctive national peculiarities." He believed that racial purity and isolation bred national retrogression; interracial mingling and assimilationism bred national progression. He completely agreed with Dr. James McCune Smith, his black colleague, that "our great nation, so distinguished for industry and enterprise, is largely indebted to its composite character." Although the mulatto symbolized the ideal of a composite American racial character drawing upon America's component races, the white Anglo-Saxon Protestant symbolized the dominant and conflicting perception of a narrow American cultural character drawing principally upon the Anglo-European heritage. The facts of dominant white American cultural provincialism and white racism contradicted the ideal of American racial cosmopolitanism. Douglass's theoretical distinction between cultural hierarchy and racial equality did represent an attack upon racism, but his adherence to white cultural hegemony undercut the attack.

Douglass certainly had no trouble distinguishing between the ideal and the reality of the United States as a composite nationality. He clearly perceived that his country was no racially assimilationist haven. Ideologically, however, he could not separate the interdependent ideal and reality of a composite American nationality because his vision of Americans transcended race and encompassed humanity. He sensed, however, that his notion of a composite American nationality would not resonate among Americans as an ideal without some basis in reality. Consequently, he glossed over the discordant and continuing reality of racial and ethnic diversity with the assimilationist paradigm of a singular American race. In the process, he obscured America's cultural pluralism.

Taking into consideration Douglass's Anglo-European cultural bias, the fundamental flaw of his composite American nationality from the perspective of nonwhites, especially blacks, was the heavy cost it entailed. As Blyden, Douglass's pan-Africanist contemporary, observed, assimilation placed the oppressed Negro in the anomalous position of identifying with and blending biologically with the white oppressor. Jumping into the melting pot to conform to Anglo-European cultural norms, as Douglass advocated, signified self-denial from Blyden's perspective as a full-blooded Negro and partial self-discovery from Douglass's as a mulatto. Most important in his vision of a composite nationality, Douglass endeavored through assimilation to resolve the deep-seated tension between Negroness and Americanness—the Negro's sense of "twoness"—in favor of the latter.

Supporting the Woman's Rights Movement

Benjamin Quarles

The movement to emancipate the slaves and to win equal rights for women have long and frequently intertwined histories. As Benjamin Quarles here demonstrates, few individuals better personified the connection between those reform campaigns than Frederick Douglass. In 1848 Douglass was the most prominent male participant in the famous Seneca Fall Convention, which publicly launched the women's rights campaign. Douglass actively supported both the abolitionist and feminist movements throughout the 1850s, and after the Civil War he became a vice president of the Equal Rights Association dedicated to winning universal suffrage. When Congress in the late 1860s debated the Fifteenth Amendment to grant the vote to black males, a rupture occurred in the suffrage movement when many women, led by Elizabeth Cady Stanton and Susan B. Anthony, protested their sex being left behind. Many decades-old friendships between veteran abolitionists and feminists were broken. Douglass remained one of the few leaders determined to heal the wounds between old comrades and for the remainder of his life made winning the vote for women a major goal of his reform activity.

In certain districts in the South Carolina elections of 1870 colored women, under the encouragement of Negro election officials, exercised the privilege of voting. By this act the Negro became the first practical vindicator of woman's right to the ballot. This development followed the logic of events; the beginnings of the struggle for woman's rights in the United

Benjamin Quarles, "Frederick Douglass and the Woman's Rights Movement," *Journal of Negro History*, vol. 25, January 1940, pp. 35–44.

States was closely related to the anti-slavery movement. Negro leaders in their efforts to undermine legal and political institutions prejudical to their group made common cause with the handful of militant women who sought for their sex the status of complete equality in marriage, equal rights in property and wages, the right to make contracts, to sue and be sued, to testify in court and, above all, to vote.

In their early efforts to convert a hostile and jeering public the feminists received much support from colored abolitionists. Of these Negroes, among whom were Charles Lenox Remond, James McCune Smith, William Wells Brown and Robert Purvis, none was more zealous than Frederick Douglass. As soon as he had established himself at Rochester in 1847 he identified himself with the budding movement. "Right is of no sex," ran the opening phrase of Douglass' *North Star*, the first issue of which appeared in December, 1847.

ABOLITIONIST SUPPORT OF WOMAN'S RIGHTS

In July of the following year the first organized gathering for equal rights—the famous Seneca Falls Convention—was held. Of the thirty-two men who ran the risk of being branded "Aunt Nancy men," "hermaphrodites" and with similar epithets, Douglass alone was prominent in the deliberations. He was the only man who supported the resolution of Elizabeth Cady Stanton that women should vote. *The North Star* commented favorably on the convention. The proceedings "were characterized by marked ability and dignity." The editor bade the movement his humble Godspeed. The success of the meeting heartened its sponsors; they continued the sessions in Rochester on August 2. Although Douglass was not made chairman as Lucretia Mott and Mrs. Stanton advised, he was active in the work of the convention. Editorially he reiterated "that the only true basis of right was the capacity of individuals."

The first national woman's rights convention was organized toward the close of 1850. Douglass, who was in Massachusetts during October, denouncing the Fugitive Slave Law, so arranged his schedule as to be in Worcester during the third week of the month. At this historic convention representatives from nine states responded to the call to consider "the question of Woman's Rights, Duties and Relations." In attendance along with Douglass were many other uncompromising abolitionists, among them [William Lloyd]

Garrison, Wendell Phillips, S.S. Foster and Sojourner Truth.

As their movement gained momentum the women continued to find Douglass a valuable co-worker. He attended many of their state conventions and *The North Star* and *Frederick Douglass' Paper* gave notices of their conventions and the subsequent proceedings. Meetings of Negro associations in which Douglass took part invariably placed themselves on record against discrimination on account of sex. A national convention of Colored Freemen at Cleveland in 1848, with Douglass presiding, passed a resolution affirming belief in the equality of the sexes and inviting the women present to participate in the deliberations. Eight weeks later at Philadelphia, Douglass was one of the organizers of a convention of colored people at which a similar invitation was extended to women, white as well as colored. This broad stand impelled Lucretia Mott to attend the sessions. Douglass was chairman of the Committee on Declaration of Sentiments at a Colored National Convention at Rochester in July, 1853, with representatives from eight states. One of the delegates to this convention, at which "not a word of nonsense was talked," was a woman—a Mrs. Jeffrey, of Geneva. The attendance of a woman delegate was in advance of the times, but "we had the good sense to make no fuss about it," wrote Douglass.

In 1860 the Radical Abolitionists, a handful of die-hard reformers, held a convention at Worcester to consider the feasibility of organizing a party on uncompromisingly antislavery grounds. Douglass served on the executive committee. This convention invited women to participate in the proceedings. Thus was initiated the first effort ever made "to organize a political party upon a basis of absolute justice and perfect equality."

During the war the abolitionists and the feminists dropped their distinctive characters and identified themselves with the mass of citizens pledged to the support of the Union. The women of the North expended their energies in the activities of the Sanitary Commission and the National Loyal League. Douglass served the latter organization by lecturing for their cause at half his usual fee.

DISPUTE OVER VOTING RIGHTS

Reconstruction placed a severe strain on the amicable relations between those who placed first the interests of the Negro and those to whom woman's rights were paramount. The true reformers (as distinguished from those who were interested in Negro ballots as a political necessity) were advocates of impartial suffrage, but immediately after the war the inescapable question presented itself, Is it more important that Negroes should vote than that women should vote? Mrs. Stanton and Miss Anthony, more concerned with the woman question than any other cause, sought to link the political enfranchisement of their sex to the movement for male Negro suffrage. In May, 1866, these indefatigable feminists changed the Woman's Rights Convention into an Equal Rights Association, whose chief aim was universal suffrage. Douglass was chosen one of the three vice-presidents.

The issue was joined from that date. Later in the year at an Albany meeting, attended by Remond, William Wells Brown and Frances E.W. Harper, Douglass warned the Equal Rights Association that it was in danger of becoming a woman's rights association. To women the ballot was desirable, to the Negro it was vital. "With us disfranchisement means New Orleans, it means Memphis, it means New York mobs.". . .

By the middle of 1868 the women had become embittered at the slow progress of their movement. A Negro had delivered a sermon in the House of Representatives, the Civil Rights Bill had been passed, Negroes in the District of Columbia had been enfranchised and the Fourteenth Amendment was on the point of ratification. The Republican party was promoting the Negro's interests, but where, ran the women's plea, could their cause find such a champion? An explosion occurred in New York at the second anniversary of the Equal Rights Association. Douglass attempted to placate the aroused feelings of the Stantonites. After a reminder of his long advocacy of their rights, he begged them to hold their claims in abeyance. To the Negro, he reiterated, the ballot was "an urgent necessity.". . .

The parting of the ways was reached at the annual meeting of the Equal Rights Association held in New York during the second week in May, 1869. The Fifteenth Amendment was before the country, and because it contained no clause exempting sex as a basis of political discrimination, the women of the Anthony-Stanton group regarded the measure as a new affront. At the meeting the leaders of the Association, many of whom were personal friends of Douglass', listened with vexation to his familiar assertions. "When women," said Douglass, slipping into his typical style, "because they are women, are dragged from their homes and hung upon lamp-posts; when their children are torn from their arms . . . then they will have an urgency to obtain the ballot equal to black men." Many ways were open to women to redress their grievances; the Negro had but one. Loud applause greeted this rhetoric, but the majority opinion did not favor Douglass' point of view. His efforts to force through a resolution committing the Association to the support of the Fifteenth Amendment "as the culmination of one half of our demands," were unavailing. Douglass' attitude brought to the Stantonites the realization that they could not tie their movement in with Negro suffrage. Hence before the gathering disbanded the ardent feminists dissolved the Equal Rights Association and formed an organization, the National Woman's Suffrage Association, divorced entirely from the question of Negro suffrage.

The controversial amendment became law on March 30, 1870. Amid the joyous celebrations that accompanied ratification, Douglass did not forget that millions were still disfranchised because of sex. Editorially he advised colored women to prepare themselves so as to be ready to vote when a sixteenth amendment, removing their disability, should become part of the law of the land.

DOUGLASS FOR VICE PRESIDENT

During the campaign of 1872 Douglass was on a ticket for Vice-President of the United States with a woman nominee as President. The circumstances resulted wholly from the efforts of the unconventional Victoria Woodhull, who by 1870 had added woman's rights to her extremely varied enthusiasms. In the spring of 1872 Mrs. Woodhull persuaded Mrs. Stanton to use the National Woman's Suffrage Association as the sponsor of a People's Convention for the formation of a new political party. Mrs. Stanton was severely criticized shortly after for identifying the national organization with Mrs. Woodhull, but the step had been taken. In the same city and one day after the convening of the Woman's Suffrage Association, Mrs. Woodhull's tatterdemalion [rag tag] followers, 668 strong, organized The National Radical Reformers' Party, and nominated their leader by acclamation. A running mate was selected within an hour. After considering several possibilities, among them Ben Wade, Robert Dale

Owen, Theodore Tilton and Wendell Phillips, the choice of the convention finally settled on Douglass, "who was eulogized by half a dozen speakers in succession."

Mrs. Woodhull was formally notified of her nomination on the third of June. Two days later she accepted. Similar action from Douglass was not forthcoming. He completely ignored the wholly impractical, hastily extemporized movement, thereby bearing out the sentiment of Oliver Johnson, who wrote to Garrison as the convention adjourned that "Douglass will take the earliest opportunity to disclaim all connections with such a body, the proceedings of which were beneath contempt." Doubtless it was well that Douglass declined the honor. . . .

REFORM RANKS HEAL

After 1872 as the internal bickerings of the Reconstruction era died out, the woman's movement made rapid headway against a less reluctant public opinion. Douglass, happy in the prestige attaching to a pioneer in a cause becoming respectable by success, maintained a keen, consistent interest. At a moment's notice he could speak on the subject. Unless absent from Washington in January, he was a conspicuous figure at every annual convention of the National Suffrage Association.

Reunions found him on the platform. He was on the committee on arrangements of the thirtieth anniversary of the Seneca Falls Convention. Held at the same site in Rochester that had been the scene of the 1848 gathering, this was the last woman's rights assembly ever attended by the aging Mrs. Mott. The audience was moved by Douglass' heartfelt "Goodbye, dear Lucretia," as the great reformer, after a parting prophecy of triumph, moved down the aisle on her nephew's arm. Ten years later at the fortieth anniversary, held in Washington, Douglass and Mrs. Stanton were the main speakers at the session in commemoration of the pioneers. . . .

Douglass' relations with the two surviving pioneers became very cordial again after the "Negro's hour vs. woman's hour" question became a dead issue. Mrs. Stanton, reaffirming her personal esteem, was highly indignant with those who criticized Douglass' choice for his second wife. The following year in celebration of her seventieth birthday she invited Douglass to express his friendship in a letter to the *New Era*, whose entire November issue was to be devoted to her.

Miss Anthony presented him with autographed copies of the first three volumes of a history of the suffrage movement. She remained with his widow all through the day following his death. Five days later she was one of the eulogists at memorial services held at the Central Presbyterian Church in the city where they had been fellow-Rochesterians for a quarter of a century.

The bronze effigy of Douglass in the same city—the only public statue of a Negro in the United States—drew characteristic reactions from these militant reformers. Mrs. Stanton regretted that the monument did not "take the form of a schoolhouse for colored children, or a model tenement house for colored families." Shafts of stone were useless "when humanity is in need of so many ameliorations." Strong-minded Miss Anthony wondered at the grave mistake made in the placing of the statue. Douglass "always faced the North and I do not like to see him looking back to the South." She would "endeavor to have it changed."

Frederick Douglass and American Diplomacy in the Caribbean

Merline Pitre

From July 1889 to August 1891, Frederick Douglass
served as the U.S. ambassador to the Caribbean nation of Haiti. Douglass had a keen interest in the success of Haiti as the world's first black republic. At the
same time, he represented the desire of the Benjamin Harrison administration to extend U.S. influence over the Caribbean. While Douglass initially
participated in negotiations to purchase a naval coaling base from the Haitians, he ultimately balked at a
plan to use force to acquire that station and resigned
his diplomatic post. Merline Pitre, professor of history and former dean of the College of Arts and Sci-
ences at Texas Southern University, has carefully analyzed Douglass's diplomatic career. Pitre discovers
Douglass torn between his loyalty to the Republican
administration that had appointed him and his support for black Haitian self-determination. She concludes that Douglass fully embraced the rationale for
asserting America's influence over weaker neighbors
but refused to sanction territorial acquisitions without the consent of the affected country.

After 1844, the island of Santo Domingo, which now bears
the name Haiti, was divided into two independent states, the
Dominican Republic and the Republic of Haiti. The next fifty
years witnessed periods during which efforts were made to
annex the island or parts of it to the United States. While
these attempts . . . to acquire a naval base in Haiti were of vital interest to blacks of both the West Indies and the United
States, they were of special interest to the freedom fighter,
politician, and diplomat, Frederick Douglass. . . .

Merline Pitre, "Frederick Douglass and American Diplomacy in the Caribbean," *Journal of Black Studies*, vol. 13, June 1983, pp. 457, 467–73. Copyright © 1983 by Sage Pub-
lications, Inc. Reproduced by permission.

In trying to understand [Douglass's position] several factors should be taken into consideration. First, Douglass was a "self-made man" who, to a certain degree, believed in rugged individualism and social Darwinism (though he never used the terms). As a former slave, Douglass came to accept the premise that "only in America could one move from such lowly status to occupy a place in government." Second, Douglass had been educated in the abolitionist school—a school that considered Western civilization infinitely superior to other civilizations and cultures. Third, in the Republican party, Douglass was associated with individuals who advocated not only manifest destiny, but also the idea of carrying the "white man's burden" to other parts of the world. Though association with Republicans did not necessarily make Douglass an apostle of manifest destiny, Douglass sincerely believed that liberty and equality had become the law of the land under the Republican administration and thus was for extending American dominion abroad.

NEGOTIATING WITH HAITI

Given the above argument, it is not surprising that Douglass sympathized with the imperialist aspiration of Benjamin Harrison's administration for acquiring a naval base in Haiti in 1889. The argument that he used [was that] so long as slavery persisted in the United States, Douglass opposed or would have opposed expansion at black Haitians' expense. With slavery overthrown, the cardinal objection to American expansion disappeared. As such, Douglass saw no reason to oppose the *raison d'être* of his mission when he was appointed diplomat to Haiti in 1889. While primarily political in intent, Douglass's appointment was expected to facilitate the transaction of a coaling station at the Mole St. Nicolas. No doubt an overview of the negotiation for this port will shed some light on Douglass's role and/or view of American foreign policy in this area.

At no time from Ambassador Douglass's arrival in Haiti, on October 15, 1889, to November 30, 1889, was he instructed to negotiate for the Mole. Apparently his first knowledge of the United States' efforts to acquire the Mole came from reports that he had read in the newspaper in December 1889. At that time, he reported to Secretary of State J. Gordon Blaine that rumors in the American press concerning the alleged desire of the United States to acquire the

Mole, coupled with the reconnoitering of unauthorized warships in Haitian water, were creating suspicion among the Haitians. "There is a feeling," he argued in a letter to Blaine, "that preliminary steps had been taken to sell the country to the Americans." In this same letter Douglass expressed doubts over the United States' intention as perceived by the Haitians. However, he would later discover that he was deceived by protocol. Not only did Blaine know the reasons why the United States' ships were at the Mole, but he was also aware that William P. Clyde, a shipping magnate from New York, would seek the support of Douglass in order to promote his business interests in Haiti.

Not even a month had passed from the time that Blaine received the above dispatch when Clyde's agent, E.C. Reed, called upon Douglass to help him in procuring a concession from Haitian President Louis Modestin Florvil Hyppolite. This grant called for a subsidy of a half million dollars to establish a steamship line between New York and seven Haitian ports. Later on it would include a lease of the Mole St.

Nicolas for ninety-nine years. Initially, Douglass approved of the idea of the steamship line. However, he found Reed's method distasteful. Reed wanted Douglass to use his office to persuade the Haitian officials that if they would grant this concession to Clyde, he (the minister) would not press the claims of other private American citizens. This Douglass refused to do.

After the Reed incident, Douglass applied for a leave of absence, and it was not until he returned to Haiti in December 1890 that he was given verbal instruction to begin negotiation for the Mole. But now, as in the past, he did not object to his assignment. He did not even protest when he was demoted as a main negotiator for the Mole and was replaced by Rear Admiral Brancroft Gherardi. As a matter of fact, following the order of his government, he cooperated with Gherardi and made an appointment for the two of them to call upon the Haitian president and foreign minister to make a request for the Mole.

At this historic conference, Gherardi, serving as the main spokesman for the U.S. government, reminded the Haitian officials of the services the United States had rendered to their government. In other words, had it not been for the U.S. Navy, Hyppolite would not be in power. The admiral made it clear that this help was given in return for the Mole and that the United States had kept its part of the bargain; now it was time for Haiti to do likewise. When it came Douglass's turn to speak, he based his argument on what he called the diplomacy of advance civilization. He tried to impress upon the Haitian government that the concession asked for "was in the line of good neighborhood . . . that National isolation was a policy of the past, that the necessity of it in Haiti no longer exists." Douglass avoided the argument made by Gherardi that a bargain had been made between the United States and Hyppolite's government, because he was aware that it implicated the United States in an unsavory intervention. Rather, Douglass chose to support the concession by pointing out to the Haitians that such a naval station was essential to her progress.

Despite the arguments of both Gherardi and Douglass, the negotiation for the Mole St. Nicolas failed. It failed for three of several reasons: (1) because a restrictive clause in the agreement was a violation of the Haitian constitution—that is to say, this clause prohibited Haiti from "leasing any part of the island so long as the United States was the leasee of the Mole"; (2) because seven U.S. warships were hovering off the Haitian coast at the time of the negotiation; and (3) because of the dubious strategy of applying for the Clyde concession ahead of the Mole.

DOUGLASS DEFENDS HIS DIPLOMATIC RECORD

According to some people, the failure of the Mole St. Nicolas was due to the incompetency of the American diplomat, Frederick Douglass. Of this and other charges leveled at him, Douglass in some way vindicated himself by writing his "Inside History" of the negotiation for the Mole in the September and October issues of the *North American Review*. Douglass argued in no uncertain terms that he had been used by his government. Historians have generally accepted the story told by Douglass as the truthful version of his part of the Mole affair. Consequently, there has been a tendency on the part of some of them to picture Douglass as a hero rising above or blocking an immoral American foreign policy. Speaking in this vein, T. Thomas Fortune said, "The whole criticism that can be brought against Douglass' ministry is that he utterly refused to be diplomatic and to this, we his people say 'Amen.'" But this is only a half-truth. It obscures a distinction Douglass made between public and private ends. He did not believe in the use of force, or the threat of force, to acquire the Mole. But he did not try to block the lease of the Mole. In fact he worked hard to promote it.

To be sure, Douglass was an expansionist, and he was in favor of extending American influence in Haiti if it could be done to the advantage of both countries and by mutual consent. He made this clear when responding to writers who said he was indifferent to the acquisition of the Mole:

> When some of these writers were in their petticoats, I had comprehended the value of such an acquisition, both in respect to American commerce and to American influence. The policy of obtaining such a station is not new. I supported General Grant's idea on this subject against the powerful opposition of my honored and revered friend Charles Sumner. . . . I said that it was a shame to American statesmanship that while almost every other great nation in the world has secured a foothold and had power in the Caribbean Sea . . . we, who stood at the very gate of that sea, had no anchoring ground anywhere. I was for the acquisition of Samano and of Santo Domingo. . . . While slavery existed, I was opposed to all such schemes for extension of American power and influ-

ence. But since its abolition, I have gone with him who goes farthest for such extension.

Douglass was in favor of a hegemonic relationship between the United States and the Caribbean islands, but what Douglass failed to realize is that while the stronger state's dominance is rarely absolute, it is often the major factor in determining the course and outcome of events within the weaker state. That is, under certain circumstances, there is a tendency for hegemonic relationship to be self-perpetuating. Once inequality becomes embedded in the structure of a relationship, only epochal events can significantly alter its term.

DOUGLASS AS A LOYAL REPUBLICAN

In sum, it can be said that several factors contributed to Douglass's stance vis-à-vis American foreign policy: (1) his concept of American mission in the world, (2) his view of the world, and (3) his loyalty to and naivete concerning the Republican party. Probably more than any other factor, the missionary impulse helps to explain much that is baffling about Douglass's behavior. In a sense, one could consider Douglass as a missionary, confident that he comprehended the peace and well-being of other countries better than the leaders of those countries themselves. This urge to do good, to render disinterested service, was so compelling that it motivated interference in the internal affairs of other nations. Moreover, as evangels of Democracy, Douglass thought that Americans could teach the people of the Caribbean how to elect good and establish stable government. Intervention was therefore rationalized in terms of rescuing his helpless friends from foreign dangers and internal disorder. . . .

As far as Douglass's view of the world is concerned, he saw the world as one divided among a few great and wealthy powers, the smaller "civilized states" of Europe and the remaining nations of the world, which he thought of as occupying distinctive lower positions on a scale of less desirable qualities. Among these nations, he saw an unrestrained international competition. The great powers were the civilized powers, the purveyors of enlightenment and culture, the protectors of law, order, and liberty, and, to a certain extent, the practitioners of democracy.

Moreover, Douglass was a Republican party loyalist when he espoused such expansionist views. To the Republican party experiment, he was totally committed. It was only natural that this loyalty would embrace the party's foreign policy. But American foreign policy, even under the Republican administrations, was not always in keeping with the principles of justice and equality. Even if Douglass realized this, by this time his fidelity to the party had produced a myopia that permitted foreign policies to be seen only dimly. Thus it can be said that as far as American diplomacy in the Caribbean is concerned, Douglass confused a short-term objective (ascendancy of the Republican party) with a long-range goal of the peoples in the West Indies, the right to self-determination.

The Douglasses Abroad

Philip S. Foner

One of the personal highlights of Frederick Douglass's later years was his extensive travel in Europe and North Africa in 1886–1887 with his second wife Helen. He had the opportunity to renew friendships in Great Britain with aging colleagues from the abolitionist movement. The Douglasses also toured France, Italy, and Greece, encountering little of the racial prejudice that an interracial couple endured in the United States of that era. The most exciting stop for Douglass was in Egypt where he scaled the pyramid of Cheops and observed the functioning of a racially diverse society. The following account of the Douglasses' tour is excerpted from a biography of Douglass by the late Philip S. Foner, a prodigious author of books in labor and African American history.

Almost thirty years had passed since Douglass made his last trip to Europe. At that time he had fled to England for refuge, an outlaw hunted by the government because of his connections with John Brown. Now he went as a man who had known presidents, senators, and congressmen. His letters of introduction to prominent Europeans likened him to "Abraham Lincoln, Garfield, Charles Sumner and Wendell Phillips." "Few men can tell more of American history for the last-half century than Mr. Douglass can, and no one has been able to see it from the same point of view," went one letter of introduction.

After a week's sailing, the couple arrived in Liverpool. Douglass found "everything about the Docks the same as forty years ago except forty years older and by reason of smoke darker." The people were "full of life and activity."

During the week's stay in Liverpool, the Douglasses visited art galleries, the Free Library, and the exhibition of new paintings. They also spent a day on the *Great Eastern*, "that

Philip S. Foner, *Frederick Douglass.* New York: The Citadel Press, 1950. Copyright © 1950 by International Publishers Co., Inc. Reproduced by permission.

wonder of Naval architecture . . . now used as a show and a low class of Theatricals."

On October 1, the couple left for St. Neots "to spend a few days there before going to London." Here they were met by Julia Griffiths Crofts "with open arms." Twenty-six years had passed since Julia and Douglass had seen one another, and the five day stay at St. Neots was filled with reminiscences. Julia's husband had died ten years before and she now supported herself by running a school for girls. Douglass addressed the children at Julia's request.

THE DOUGLASSES IN FRANCE

After two weeks in London, the Douglasses left for Paris. With Theodore Stanton, son of Elizabeth Cady Stanton, and Theodore Tilton as their guides, the couple visited the interesting places in Paris.

Deeply impressed by a visit to the Bastille, Douglass wrote to his son Lewis, urging him to "read of the manner in which it was taken in your cyclopedia." He added:

> I find the people here singularly conscious of their liberty, independence and their power. They show it in their whole carriage and in the very lines of their faces, and no wonder, for they, more than any other people in Europe, have asserted all three in the face of organized oppression and power. But in no act have they done this more than in their taking the Bastille.

Douglass was moved by the culture and art about him, with one exception: the statue of Alexander Dumas left him cold. On meeting eighty-two-year-old Victor Schoelcher, the senator who had drawn up the law emancipating the slaves in the French colonies, Douglass had spoken to him of the elder Dumas. He had learned that the famous writer had "never said one word for his race."

"So we have nothing to thank Dumas for," Douglass wrote to friends in America.

> Victor Hugo the white man could speak for us, but this brilliant colored man who could have let down sheets of fire upon the heads of tyrants and carried freedom to his enslaved people, had no word in behalf [of] Liberty or the enslaved. I have not yet seen his statue here in Paris. I shall go to see it, as it is an acknowledgement of the genius of a colored man, but not because I honor the character of the man himself.

In Paris a few weeks, Douglass began to see himself as the unofficial ambassador of the American Negro. He felt that his presence "even in silence, has a good influence in respect of the colored race before the world." The mass of the people in England and France were "sound in their convictions and feelings concerning the colored race." But "the lepros distilment of the American prejudice against the Negro" was having its effect in Europe. In part, it was caused by "Ethiopian singers [from America] who disfigure and distort the features of the Negro and burlesque his language and manners in a way to make him appear to thousands as more akin to apes than to men"—a "mode of warfare . . . purely American." In addition to "these Ethiopian Buffoons and serenaders who presume to represent us abroad," prejudice against the Negro was stirred by "malicious American writers who take pleasure in assailing us, as an inferior and good for nothing race of which it is impossible to make anything."

In private conversations both in England and France, Douglass sought to counteract these vicious influences. He planned to deliver a number of speeches in England "in vindication of the cause and the character of the colored race in America, in which I hope to do justice to their progress and make known some of the difficulties with which as a people they have to contend."

ITALIAN HOLIDAY

The Douglasses left Paris early in January, 1887, for a trip to Rome, stopping at Dejun, Lyons, Avignon, and Marseilles. At Avignon, "one of the oldest, quaintest, crookedest and queerest places" he had ever seen, Douglass visited the ancient Palaces of the Popes. When he peered into the dungeons "where people were tortured and doomed to death for rejecting the Roman faith," Douglass' critical attitude toward organized religion asserted itself. "I almost hated the name of church," he confided to his diary. "What a horrible lie that Romish church has palmed of[f] upon the people of this and other country pretending that its Pope is the Vice regent of God, the creator of the Universe, and how strange it is that millions of sane men have believed this stupendous and most arrogant lie."

The diary Douglass kept during his stay in Rome contained much of his resentment over the contradictions between the theory and practice of Christianity. The splendor of the dome of St. Peters, the largest cathedral in the world, evoked his admiration, but he noted "its utter contradiction to the life and lessons of Jesus. He was meek and lowly, but here was little else than pride and pomp." Through the intervention of Mrs. E.J. Putnam who was a friend of "an eminent priest," the Douglasses were able to see some of the "interior treasures" of St. Peters. Douglass' anger mounted as he examined the "costly vestments" decorated with gold and silver, rich laces "and all manner of precious stones worn by Popes, Cardinals, Bishops," the gold and silver crosses, and "other brilliant things with which [the] papacy well knows how to dazzle the eyes of the credulous and superstitious."

> The sight of these things only increased my sense of the hollowness of the vast structure of the Romish church and my conviction that Science must in the end do for that church what time has done for the vast structures of kingly pride and power which is broken and mouldering all over Rome. . . .

The couple walked on the Appian way, strolled on Pincian Hill, and viewed the ruins of the Coliseum and the Forum. Leaving Rome late in January, they were delighted by the trip to Naples, especially the view of the snow clad Appenines "with their changing forms and lofty heights." Before arriving in Naples, they were entranced by the "wondrous spectacle" of Mt. Vesuvius. The sight, Douglass wrote, "almost paid us for our voyage across the sea," and "held us in almost breathless interest, and became more imposing and impressive the longer we beheld it."

They spent three days in Naples, visiting the Bourbon Palace and its beautiful grounds and dining on the shore of the river Styx. They saw the landing place of Paul, the tomb of Virgil, and the home of Cicero. "It was a day long to be remembered," Douglass noted.

> That which interested me most was the fact that I was looking upon the country seen eighteen hundred years ago by the Prisoner Apostle on his way to Rome to answer for his religion. It somehow gave me a more vivid impression of the heroism of the man as I looked upon the grand ruins of the religion against which Paul dared to preach. These heathen Temples represent a religion as sincerely believed in as men now believe in the Christian religion, and Paul was an infidel to this heathen religion as much as Robert Ingersol[l] is now to the Christian religion.

After a day of rest, the couple viewed the ruins of Pompeii. It was "almost worth the voyage across the Atlantic to see the part of Pompeii already unearthed and to think of the two thirds of it still underground." Douglass was quick to note that the Pompeians had been "wealthy and powerful slaveholders."

On Sunday, February 6, Douglass listened to a sermon in Italian at the Methodist church. Called upon to say a few words, which were interpreted by Reverend Jones, Douglass congratulated the congregation for having acquired "the Liberty to worship outside the Romish church and said a few words of human brotherhood."

SPIRITUAL RETURN TO AFRICA

A visit to Amalfi gave Douglass "the greatest treat of all"—a ride upon a donkey to the Capuchin convent. After viewing the celebrated Temple of Neptune built 7000 years before the birth of Christ, the couple returned to Naples. Here on February 11, they decided to extend their tour to Egypt and Greece. "The thought of this trip to Egypt and Greece will probably keep me awake tonight," Douglass wrote excitedly. "This tour is entirely outside of my calculation when leaving home, but it will be something to contemplate when it is done. It is no small thing to see the land of Joseph and his brethren, and from which Moses led the children of Abraham out of the home of bondage." He remembered how often this story had stirred him when he was a slave, how often it had lifted his spirits when he thought he was doomed to live forever in bondage.

On February 13, the couple boarded the ship for Port Said. Douglass could not refrain from reflecting "that born as I was a slave marked for a life under the lash in the cornfield that [I] was abroad and free and privileged to see these distant lands so full of historic interest and which those of the most highly favored by fortune are permitted to visit." The February 14 item in his diary opened: "If right in my estimate of the length of time I have been in the world, I am now 70 years old."

Two days later, they arrived at Port Said, "the queerest of queer places." As the Arab laborers carried baskets of coal on board the ship, Douglass was astonished by the "strength, cheerfulness and endurance of these sable children of the desert." He was quick to notice "several genuine Negroes among them," and commented that "they seemed not a whit behind their fellow workmen either in poise or physical ability."

The voyage down the Suez Canal to Ismalia was through barren and desolate country. At Ismalia Douglass saw a Greek patriarch in a flowing robe, and his objection to outward manifestations of religious beliefs came to the surface immediately. "I find it hard to look with patience upon people who thus parade their religion in their clothes, and who evidently wish to exact homage on account of such pretention," he wrote.

From Ismalia they traveled through the "Bible famous Land of Goshen" where everything reminded Douglass of "the days of Moses." The great mass of the people, he noted, would in America "be classed with mulattoes." But he quickly added that "this would not be a scientific description, but an American description." He saw now why the Mohammedan religion appealed to these people, "for it does not make color the criterion of fellowship as some of our so called Christian nations do."

In Cairo Douglass was depressed by the "squalor, disease and deformity—all manner of unfortunate beggary." But even "more pitiful" than the sight of a people "thus groveling in filth and utter wretchedness" was the daily encounter with "hooded and veiled women." He remarked: "It is sad to think of that one-half of the human family should be thus cramped, kept in ignorance and degraded, having no existence except that of minister[ing] to the pride and lusts of the men who own them as slaves are owned. . . ."

Douglass was also distressed by the sight of the Howling Dervishes at worship. The frenzy and the shouting saddened him. He could not understand how rational beings "could be made to believe that such physical contortions could be pleasing to God or secure his favour." This led him to reflect on the "form of worship adopted by many other denominations." He marveled that "man should imagine to secure Divine favor by telling God how good and great he is—and how much they love and adore him."

But there were more pleasant experiences in Egypt: the twelve-mile trip to the site of ancient Memphis; the visit to Gizeh and the 470-foot climb to the top of Cheops, the highest pyramid in the Valley of the Nile. It was a difficult and dangerous undertaking, and only with the aid of four Arabs was Douglass able to reach the top. It took him two weeks to recover, and he vowed that he would not undertake it again "for any consideration." But the view of the Sphinx, the Nile and the desert, compensated him for his aches and pains.

Early in March, the couple left Cairo and took a five-day trip up the Nile to Alexandria. Douglass left the boat with a clear understanding of the importance of the river to the Egyptians. It was to them, he now saw, "the source of life and whatever of health and prosperity they enjoyed."

AMID CLASSICAL RUINS

From Alexandria they moved on to Athens. Douglass felt excited as he paced the deck of the Egyptian steamer. "The thought of soon treading the classic shores of Greece is very exhilarating," he exclaimed. For twelve days the exhilaration mounted as the Douglasses visited the Acropolis, the Parthenon, the theatre of Dionysus, the Temple of Jupiter, and ascended by a zigzag path to the top of Lycabettis, 919 feet above sea level. As he looked down, Douglass saw "a scene never to be forgotten."

> The Plains of Attica were spread out at our feet. Over the mountain we could almost see the fields of Marathon, off towards the sea we could see clearly the Mountains of Sparta. In the city of Athens, solemn and grand with its many pillars— stood out the form of the Temple of Theseus one of the most perfect and striking of all the fallen architectural ruins left to tell us the wealth, pride, ambition, and power of the ancient people of this famous city.

Leaving Athens, the couple spent two weeks at Naples and then returned to Rome. Here they witnessed the colorful Easter services at St. Peters which Douglass described as "abounding in excellent music, much kneeling, changing of vestments, much posturing, making signs of the cross, and which seemed to my eyes mere pantomime but which to the worshippers I must try to believe was full of devotion." The glaring contrasts between wealth and poverty in Rome deepened Douglass' belief that that religion was best which best served the interests of the mass of the people on earth. Here in Rome, he pointed out, one found a "city of divinity and dirt, of Religion and rags, of grandeur and squalor, piety and poverty, of church bells and beggars, of lofty domes, towers and turrets pointing to heaven, and of dark cavernous rooms never reached by pure air or sunshine, crowded with the poor and diseased." Douglass favored less religion and fewer rags, less piety and fewer poor, fewer churches and more pure air and sunshine for the poverty-stricken. . . .

After a month at Rome, the Douglasses arrived in Florence. During the five days of sightseeing, the couple visited the Uffizi Palace, the Church of San Marco, the grand mausoleum of the Medici, and the tombs built by Michelangelo. They left for Venice feeling that their stay in Florence had been "all too brief."

Venice where "climate, sea, and sky" were beautiful surpassed "all the ideas" Douglass had formed of it. It was in many respects "the most beautiful" of all the cities they had visited. At the "Bibliotec" Douglass saw the original manuscripts of letters from John Adams, Thomas Jefferson, and Benjamin Franklin. On the great canal, he saw the house where Desdemona lived when wooed by Othello.

After Venice came Milan which "aside from its splendid Cathedral" was "not remarkable," Lucerne with its "beautiful lake," and then Paris again. Arriving on May 25, they remained only five days. Before he left Douglass called again on Senator Schoelcher. "In parting with [the] venerable Senator he kissed me on both cheeks," Douglass confided to his diary.

Early in June, Helen left for America to be with her mother who was seriously ill. Douglass remained in the British Isles for two more months, visiting old friends, giving an occasional lecture, and seeing some of the sights he had missed during previous visits. He returned to the United States in August, 1887.

MISSED IN HIS ABSENCE

It had been a memorable trip. His reaction to many of the things he had seen was fairly typical of the average tourist. But as a Negro in the old world he also saw things which were ignored by most travelers. His observations on the attitude of the common people toward men and women of color were significant. He himself had been happy to get away from the color line, to "walk the world unquestioned, a man among men." But he was especially stimulated by the knowledge that his people had missed him and welcomed his safe return. As one young Negro wrote in his letter of welcome:

> The loss of your presence and the opportunity to consult you in important matters that concerned our welfare were keenly felt by your many friends and the colored people generally:— by your absence we were made more fully to appreciate our great advantage in having you to speak for us and protect our interests.

Triumphant Days at the World's Columbian Exposition

Anna R. Paddon and Sally Turner

Douglass's retirement from his diplomatic post in Haiti did not end his involvement with that small Caribbean nation. When the international World's Columbian Exposition opened in Chicago to mark the four hundredth anniversary of Columbus's first trip to the New World, the Haitian government engaged Douglass to serve as its exhibit's commissioner. Douglass used his prominent post at the Columbian exposition as a platform to issue well-publicized attacks on the growing problems of racial segregation and lynching in the southern United States. As two journalism professors, Anna R. Paddon of Southern Illinois University and Sally Turner of Emporia State University, observe in the following selection, the exposition also gave Douglass the opportunity to meet and influence many younger African Americans who would represent their race in the next century.

The flamboyant World's Columbian Exposition, an international celebration in Chicago of the 400th anniversary of Columbus's voyage, had been open for just two weeks in 1893 when the first in a series of international congresses— the Congress of Representative Women—opened and Frederick Douglass made an unscheduled statement. He had been sitting on the platform listening to addresses and responses on the general topic of "The Solidarity of Human Interests." After several European and Canadian speakers, three black women discussed the "Progress of Women of African Descent in the United States." In her speech, Fannie Jackson Coppin, who had been a slave until an aunt bought her freedom for $175 and who then received a college education, argued for providing higher education for women. After Coppin finished, the audience pressed Douglass to speak. He said:

> I have heard to night what I hardly expected ever to live to hear. I have heard refined, educated colored ladies addressing—and addressing successfully—one of the most intelligent white audiences that I ever looked upon. It is the new thing under the sun, and my heart is too full to speak; my mind is too much illuminated with hope and with expectation for the race in seeing this sign.

> Dear friends, I am full and you are full. You have heard more tonight that you will remember, perhaps, but the grand spirit which has proceeded from this platform will live in your memory and work in your lives always.

However, just months before, Douglass had expressed disappointment and anger about the fair in his introduction of fellow-journalist Ida B. Wells's booklet, *The Reason Why the Colored America Is Not in the World's Columbian Exposition.* This publication, intended to inform international visitors about the snub African Americans received from government and fair officials, included the charge from Douglass that slavery was the reason that blacks were excluded from participation in the fair administration and exhibits. He pointed out that this was only an extension of the exclusion African Americans experienced in society.

Before the fair opened, his remarks about the dedication ceremonies were equally pessimistic. Douglass pointed out that no blacks had been invited to join the dignitaries on the main platform.

> In contemplating the inauguration ceremonies, glorious as they were, there was one thing that dimmed their glory. . . . I saw, or thought I saw, an intentional slight to that part of the American population with which I am identified.

This gloom contrasted with the optimism he expressed after the fair opened as he witnessed the intellectual and artistic accomplishments of African Americans in a variety of world congresses and informal contacts. His appointment as a commissioner from Haiti gave him the role of elder statesman, foreign diplomat, and encourager of the new generation of African American leadership. With his oratory, he championed human rights and equality.

DOUGLASS ON THE MEANING OF HAITI

In January 1893, his first major speech of the fair was at the dedication of the Haitian pavilion, one of many international pavilions used to highlight each country's history and accomplishments. Haiti, celebrating the ninetieth anniversary of its independence, saw the fair as an opportunity to display its progress to an international audience. Douglass, who had served as ambassador to Haiti a few years earlier, was chosen as Haiti's spokesman; his appointment as a commissioner demonstrated that country's regard for him. Choosing Douglass was a wise move, as he received the publicity that fair management failed to give the country. At the dedication of Haiti's pavilion, for example, the fair's director-general was the only fair official in attendance. He apologized to Douglass and to the audience that no other officials were present for the ceremony, blaming lack of publicity for the oversight. However, lack of promotion did not keep local newspapers from covering the dedication. The opportunity to hear Douglass likely made the event newsworthy.

The day before the building's dedication, Douglass told an audience at the Palmer House that the Haitian Building and the country's part in the fair were "a reaffirmation of [Haiti's] existence and independence as a nation and of her place among the sisterhood of nations." At the dedication, Douglass drew parallels between the struggle of the Haitians and of African Americans since the Civil War, pointing out that Haitians, too, were slaves before winning independence. For Douglass, the success of the Haitian revolution compared to the freedom earned by those who fought in the American Revolution.

Thus, Douglass proclaimed, Haiti, a black nation ninety years strong, stood before a world audience to show it was "still free, its spirit unbroken." The nation was a symbol to African Americans and other members of the race of what could be accomplished with unity and determination. Douglass challenged the entire race to take pride in Haiti's struggle and achievements.

THE EXPOSITION AND BLACK AMERICA

As a commissioner of Haiti, Douglass had a role of political and social power. African Americans were able to see one of their own, while not honored formally by the United States, acknowledged by a world audience as a leader. Newspaper coverage of the formal reception for the Haitian pavilion included a full-length illustration of a distinguished Douglass receiving guests, as well as a detailed description of the afternoon's events, acknowledging Douglass's place in the proceedings. He touched hundreds who stopped to speak with him. In her autobiography, Ida B. Wells recalled:

> . . . whenever he went out into the grounds or visited one of the other buildings or showed himself in the reception room of the Haitian building, he was literally swamped by white persons who wanted to shake his hand, tell of some former time when they heard him speak, or narrate some instance of the anti-slavery agitation in which they or their parents had taken part with Mr. Douglass.

The fair, of course, was held at a time in the United States when African Americans, although given the right to citizenship with the Fourteenth Amendment and the right to vote with the Fifteenth Amendment, were still unsure of their place in society. However, the Fifteenth Amendment applied only to black men. While African Americans had legal rights, there were increasing hints of racial discrimination in American society. In three years, *Plessy v. Ferguson* would solidify what African Americans already knew through experience: they did not have the equality they had believed the Civil War would guarantee.

As influential African American leaders convened at the Chicago fair, they addressed these concerns as participants in the world congresses. These congresses, sometimes referred to as parliaments, were a series of off-site intellectual forums on topics like labor, religion, and women's rights. Douglass was a platform guest and spoke at several congresses. Most noteworthy were his remarks at the Women's Congress in May and at a Good Government Congress in August. Booker T. Washington, in his biography of Douglass, characterized these speeches as two of his best. He also spoke at the World's Congress on Africa later that month and was characterized in newspaper coverage as having "a witchery in his oratory."

While in attendance at the Women's Congress, for example, he was greeted "with loud evidences of admiration. He spoke a few eloquent words of eulogy upon the valiant workers for the cause for women's rights.". . .

His forty-year fight for suffrage and women's equality made Douglass a friend of Elizabeth Cady Stanton and Susan B. Anthony, and he stood beside them on the platform at their special Suffrage Congress in August. When a North Carolinian read a paper titled "Race Suffrage in the South" that argued for white supremacy, Douglass rose in rebuttal.

> He [Douglass] cut Mr. Weeks' arguments to tatters in dramatic style as he paced up and down the platform. Negroes were thought all right, he said, so long as they were tatterdemalions. It was only when they aspired to be gentlemen they were considered offensive upstarts.

Douglass also shared the platform with white suffragette and abolitionist Isabella Beecher Hooker at the Suffrage Congress and at Colored People's Day.

COLORED PEOPLE'S DAY

However, it was during the polarization of black viewpoints about Colored People's Day that Douglass exercised controversial leadership, resulting in his most moving oratory and the showcasing of the talents of others. Just as the fair had designated various days to honor other ethnic groups like the Irish and French or interest groups like stenographers and college fraternities, the fair leadership proposed a Colored People's Day for August 25. Various African American groups bitterly disagreed how best to represent themselves and gain support for social and political change. A debate raged about how the Colored Men's Protective Association should deal with the assigned Colored People's Day at the fair. Most agreed that the fair's management had not given African Americans the recognition they deserved, but how best to handle the assigned day was not as easily agreed upon. Some, like anti-lynching crusader Ida B. Wells, tried to discourage participation in the day. Others urged an all-out boycott. . . .

But it was Douglass's calm and reason that prevailed. While he certainly understood how members of his race felt about African Americans once more being treated separately from their countrymen, especially on an international stage, and acknowledged the discrimination in the United States and at the fair, he nonetheless urged dignified participation. In a meeting held to discuss the issue several days before the designated day, Douglass implored:

> . . . we are given one day at the Fair in which we may lay our case before the world. Let us take this chance. Let us not sulk, but show to the world what sort of men and women are the product of thirty years of freedom.

Indeed, Douglass wanted the finest entertainers and most learned scholars to represent the race and to showcase the accomplishments of the African American on that day when the world would be watching. Douglass worked to make the day a success. Members of his family took part in the festivities as did singers and speakers. The day was heralded a success.

DOUGLASS'S PROTÉGÉS

Poet Paul Laurence Dunbar and musician/composer Will Marion Cook also performed at Colored People's Day. Dunbar was a young poet, who at the time of the fair had published a small volume of poetry. At the fair *Oak and Ivy* came to the attention of William Dean Howells, the noted literary critic and publisher, who reviewed the book and helped Dunbar achieve national recognition. Douglass had employed Dunbar as an assistant at the Haitian pavilion, and he continued

---

THE GRAND OLD MAN AT THE FAIR

Christopher Robert Reed is Seymour N. Logan Professor of History and North American Studies at Roosevelt University. In his study of the 1892 World's Columbian Exposition, Reed notes that Douglass was troubled by the indifference that fair officials displayed toward African Americans. Nevertheless, Douglass played a prominent role at that fair, Reed finds, and used it as a forum for advocating civil rights.

First and foremost, Frederick Douglass had plans to attend the October 11, 1892, inaugural ceremonies in which he was prepared to assume the mantle of national spokesman for Afro-America. Serving as a fulcrum for both diasporan [minority] thought and action, the "grand old man" would live out his greatest triumph and culminate his life as the dominant African American personality at the exposition. A living paradox, he had become Afro-Saxon America's ambassador to the nation. Born into slavery of mixed heritage, baptized among the righteous of New England's abolitionist stalwarts, committed to the realization of the promise of a color-blind American democracy, Douglass often criticized the land of his birth but never renounced her. His unwavering adoration for the best that America offered completely overwhelmed any animosity that he held toward her many imperfections. While he forgave, he could never forget America's moral obligation to publicly profess its past sinfulness and what he grew to consider as world's fair snubs rooted in the nation's slave past.

Christopher Robert Reed, *"All the World Is Here!": The Black Presence at White City*. Bloomington: Indiana University Press, 2000.

to support and publicize Dunbar's work after the fair. Dunbar's elegy "Frederick Douglass," published after Douglass's death in 1895, revealed the sorrow felt by millions and the gratitude felt by the poet for Douglass's mentoring. Cook was musical director for Colored People's Day. Douglass had known him as a child in Washington, DC, and had recognized his musical talent. He had arranged a benefit concert so that money could be raised for Cook's study abroad.

Another protégé, journalist Wells, had already made a name for herself with her anti-lynching crusades. Not only did her work appear in Southern newspapers during the fair, but accounts of lynchings were also reported on the front page of the *Chicago Daily Inter Ocean.* Wells had enlisted Douglass's help and support with the polemic *The Reason Why the Colored American Is Not in the World's Columbian Exposition* and often sought his company during the fair. Douglass offered assistance and wrote the introduction for her book. The year following the fair, with Douglass's blessing and encouragement, she traveled to England to gain financial support for her anti-lynching campaign.

Perhaps as important as his voice of wisdom and his aid to individuals in their quest for reform was Douglass's powerful presence as a symbol of intelligence and refinement. An editorial in the *Chicago Daily Inter Ocean* noted that Douglass, had "compelled respect for blood and black faces." It held that for a race to be revered by everyone, the best of the race should represent it. "No gathering can be made ridiculous which has for its president Frederick Douglass."

DOUGLASS DEFENDS HIS RACE

While the degree of participation by leading African Americans was debated throughout the planning stages and on the day itself, the question of who best to deliver the oration was not. With the eyes of the media and of an audience of "several thousand people" upon him, Douglass delivered an address which often was interrupted by applause.

Douglass opened his remarks by acknowledging that although the fair's management had failed to recognize the role African Americans played in the growth and development of the United States as well as the accomplishments of the race, it had given black men and women "the opportunity now ... to define our position and set ourselves right before the world." Douglass intended to take advantage of that opportunity, to "protect ourselves from unfavorable inference and misrepresentation." He argued that African Americans' exclusion from the fair was a reflection of their exclusion from most necessities and luxuries afforded white Americans. He claimed that the small degree of participation of African Americans was not from "ignorance or. . .want of public spirit," but rather from the same kind of discrimination that met them in everyday life. He stated:

> That we are outside of the World's Fair is only consistent with the fact that we are excluded from every respectable calling, from workshops, manufactories and from the means of learning trades. It is consistent with the fact that we are outside of the church and largely outside of the state.

He pointed to the role African American soldiers had played in the Civil War and to the progress the race had made since being freed.

Once again his rhetoric, stature, and passion moved the crowd. The *Chicago Tribune* used poetic words and expressions in its description of the event: "Shaking his white mane and trembling with the vehemence of his eloquence the old man for more than haft an hour held 2,500 persons under a spell." Later the newspaper's account noted Douglass's strength and fury of delivery:

> The old man, his long, white hair falling about his face, leaned far over and pointed downward, all the wrongs of his race atire [sic] in his voice. A moment later he was cool and dignified again, thrusting shafts of satire . . . and holding up to ridicule the apparent inconsistencies which, he claimed, mark the treatment of the black man by the white. . . .

His speech attacked lynching and discrimination in employment. He pleaded for the recognition of constitutional rights and rejected suggestions that the only solution to what some had termed the "negro problem" was a return to Africa. "We intend that the American people shall learn the great lesson of the brotherhood of man and the fatherhood of God from our presence among them," he said.

This was the climax of his message and the pinnacle of his dignified image at the fair. The fair had given him the opportunity to keep the need for African American equality on the public agenda. After the fair Douglass continued to criticize fair management and to use its treatment of the African American as an example of treatment nationwide. . . .

However, those who spent time with Douglass during the

Chicago fair noted an expression of satisfaction and a graciousness that seemed to reflect a sense that he had accomplished his life's work. During this summer of 1893, Douglass could bask in the recollections and praise of those who sought to meet him at the Haitian pavilion. At the fair he mentored many of the emerging leaders who would shape the issues faced by African Americans in the twentieth century. The fair provided a meeting place and a forum for these new voices. Douglass was often on the platform as these younger blacks spoke, and his complimentary comments revealed delight and optimism about the role of the new leadership. He frequently arranged introductions for young blacks, which opened professional and personal doors for them.

The closing of the fair on November 1, 1893, ended Douglass's official public career. He had invested the six months of the fair to draw world attention to the achievements of his race, to remind African Americans of their heritage, and to decry both incipient and violent racism. Within fifteen months he died. The causes he championed were picked up by the next generation's leaders, many of whom had crossed paths with him at the fair.

CHAPTER 4

DEBATING THE LEGACY OF FREDERICK DOUGLASS

Final Honors and Tributes

Booker T. Washington

One of Frederick Douglass's very first biographers was Booker T. Washington, the African American educator who in many early twentieth-century minds had picked up Douglass's fallen mantle as spokesperson for their race. Washington concludes his book with the following account of Douglass's final days. While Washington praises Douglass's enduring commitment to numerous social reform campaigns, he was most laudatory about Douglass as a role model for younger blacks who continuously urged on them: "the necessity of cultivating a spirit of race pride,—of setting before themselves and the race of which they were members clear and definite ideals."

With the closing of the [world's Columbian] Exposition in the autumn of 1893, ended the last chapter in [Douglass's] life as a public official. As office-holding, however, was by no means the most important part of his career, it did not require an office to keep him in view of the people. His prominence outlasted that of many of his contemporaries who were more favored than he in the matter of public service. He remained, up to the very last hour of his life, one of the few men of the nation of whom it never tired. This was so, largely because he was more a part of the present than of the past. Though he compassed in his life over a half-century of national history, he never got out of touch with current events, retaining to the end his influence on public opinion in all those matters in which he was peculiarly interested, and in regard to which his views had special authority. . . .

The last two years of his life seem to have been more free from care and active duties than any previous period. He merited a rest and he had everything about him to contribute to his ease and enjoyment. Among the trees and

Booker T. Washington, *Frederick Douglass*. Philadelphia: George W. Jacobs, 1906.

flowers of his ample grounds on Cedar Hill, and surrounded by his books and the comforts of his classic home, life went on serenely and happily.

One of the interesting sights here was the procession of people of all kinds making pilgrimages every day to the home of "the Sage of Anacostia," as he was fondly called by his friends and neighbors. Thousands of colored persons visited him to pay their respects to the man whose life had been consecrated to the cause of their emancipation and citizenship. To all he was kindly and considerate. His mind was as alert and keen as ever, and thoroughly alive to passing events. He had a special fondness for the young men of his race, and particularly those who were educated and progressive. It was always an inspiration to him to see the numbers of young colored men, who were fitting themselves by study and application to pass civil service examinations, and gain for themselves positions of importance in all departments of the government. He frequently invited them to his home to dine with him, and would discuss with them the possibilities for their advancement in all lines of endeavor. He was always hopeful regarding the progress of these young men in business and in the professions.

He was generous, almost to a fault, with his time, money, and services in behalf of any cause that meant a step forward for his people. His health was uniformly good. Every day he was either riding or walking about the streets of Washington, or in conference with those who needed his advice and assistance in all kinds of helpful enterprises. He had a part in every civic event of any importance in the District of Columbia. No one colored man before or since his death has wielded so much influence in all directions. He had not only won the esteem of the people of Washington, but he knew how to deserve and retain it. In the District government, in the public schools, and at Howard University, his influence was felt and respected.

DOUGLASS AS A ROLE MODEL

What he himself was, he had gained by hard work, consecration, temperate habits, and God-fearing conduct toward all his fellows. His life and achievements spoke eloquently to the young men about him and pointed the way to progress. Mr. Douglass had richly earned everything that he had, and those who took him as a model were made to realize that success comes not as a gift, but must be deserved and won as a reward for right thinking and high living. Poor as were his people in all things, Frederick Douglass found enough to be proud of in them and urged continuously upon the younger generation the necessity of cultivating a spirit of race pride,—of setting before themselves and the race of which they were members clear and definite ideals.

In nothing else was the life of Mr. Douglass so important as in the uplifting influence he exerted, directly and indirectly, upon the young men of his time. There were many good leaders worthy of emulation, but none who exercised the authority that he did over the opinions of the other members of his race. His life was an open book. Naturally there were those of his color who envied him; who sought to discredit his worth and work; who felt that so long as he lived and spoke, none other could be known or heard. The young men of force and intelligence, however, who had it in them to do something large and important looked up to and were inspired by the "old man eloquent" of the Negro race.

It is easily possible to extend observations of this kind concerning the personality and influence of this great man during those restful years when he was happily free from care and public responsibilities. How little he thought of death! Sound of body and sane of mind, and always thinking and planning for what should come after, he lived as if there was no claim upon his future existence which he could not adjust. When death did come on the second day of February, 1895, it found him with no preparation, in the ordinary sense, for its message. And yet it had always been his expressed wish that he should go as he did—"to fall as the leaf in the autumn of life."

On that day he had been attending the Council of Women which was meeting in Metzerott's Hall in the city of Washington, and was much interested in the proceedings. He was an honorary member of that body. They were in quest of larger liberties for themselves, as he so long had been for himself and his people. When Frederick Douglass appeared at the convention in the morning, he was greeted with applause and escorted to the platform by a committee. He remained there nearly the entire day. When he returned to his home on Cedar Hill for dinner, he was in the best of spirits, and with a great deal of animation and pleasure, discussed with Mrs. Douglass the incidents of the meeting.

After the meal he prepared himself to deliver an address in a colored Baptist church near by. His carriage was at the door. While passing through the hall from the dining-room, he seemed to drop slowly upon his knees, but in such a way that the movement did not excite any alarm in his wife. His

---

ELIZABETH CADY STANTON ON DOUGLASS

Frederick Douglass and Elizabeth Cady Stanton worked together to advance the rights of both African Americans and women since the Seneca Falls Convention of 1848. After learning of Douglass's death in February 1895, Stanton reflected in her diary on Douglass's great talents.

Taking up the papers to-day [February 21, 1895], the first word that caught my eye thrilled my very soul. Frederick Douglass is dead! What memories of the long years since he and I first met chased each other, thick and fast, through my mind and held me spellbound. A graduate from the "Southern Institution," he was well fitted to stand before a Boston audience and, with his burning eloquence, portray his sufferings in the land of bondage. He stood there like an African prince, majestic in his wrath, as with wit, satire, and indignation he graphically described the bitterness of slavery and the humiliation of subjection to those who, in all human virtues and powers, were inferior to himself. Thus it was that I first saw Frederick Douglass, and wondered that any mortal man should have ever tried to subjugate a being with such talents, intensified with the love of liberty. Around him sat the great antislavery orators of the day, earnestly watching the effect of his eloquence on that immense audience, that laughed and wept by turns, completely carried away by the wondrous gifts of his pathos and humor. On this occasion, all the other speakers seemed tame after Frederick Douglass. In imitation of the Methodist preachers of the South, he used to deliver a sermon from the text, "Servants, obey your masters," which some of our literary critics pronounced the finest piece of satire in the English language. The last time I visited his home at Anacosta, near Washington, I asked him if he had the written text of that sermon. He answered, "No, not even notes of it." "Could you give it again?" I asked. "No," he replied; "or at least I could not bring back the old feelings even if I tried, the blessing of liberty I have so long enjoyed having almost obliterated the painful memories of my sad early days."

Theodore Stanton and Harriot Stanton Blatch, eds. *Elizabeth Cady Stanton.* New York: Arno Press, 1969.

face wore a look of surprise as he exclaimed, "Why, what does this mean!" Then, straightening his body upon the floor, he was gone. The men who responded to Mrs. Douglass's agonized cries for help, came hurriedly with physicians, but it was too late. Douglass was dead—without pain, without warning, without fear, and at a time when life was sweet, full, and complete. His last moment of enthusiasm, like his first hours of aspiration when a slave-child, was for liberty; if not for himself, then for some one else. . . .

Douglass lived long enough to see the triumph of the cause for which he had dreamed, hoped, and labored. But he had lived long enough, also, to realize that what slavery had been two hundred years and more in doing could not be wholly undone in thirty or forty years; could, in fact, hardly be wholly undone since the Future is always built out of the materials of the Past.

In his later years he came to understand that the problem, on the work of solving which he and others had entered with such high hopes in the Reconstruction period, was larger and more complicated than it at that time seemed. If the realization of this fact was a disappointment to him, it did not cause him to lose courage. His faith in the future remained unshaken. He was sane and sanguine to the end. Least of all did he allow himself to feel aggrieved or become embittered by any personal inconvenience that he encountered because of the color of his skin. . . .

Frederick Douglass's life fell in the period of war, of controversy, and of fierce party strife. The task which was assigned to him was, on the whole, one of destruction and liberation, rather than construction and reconciliation. Circumstances and his own temperament made him the aggressive champion of his people, and of all others to whom custom or law denied the privileges which he had learned to regard as the inalienable possessions of men. He was for liberty, at all times, and in all shapes. Seeking the ballot for the Negro, he was ardently in favor of granting the same privilege to woman. Holding, as he did, that there were certain rights and dignities that belong to man as man, he was opposed to discrimination in our immigration laws in favor of the white races of Europe and against the yellow races of Asia. In religion, also, he was disposed to unite himself with the extreme liberal movement. In all this he was at once an American, and a man of his time.

But Mr. Douglass was not merely an American, sharing the convictions and aspirations of the most progressive men of his day. He was also a Negro, and the lesson of his life is addressed in the most particular way to the members of his own race: "To those who have suffered in slavery, I can say, I, too, have suffered. To those who have taken some risks and encountered hardships in the flight from bondage, I can say, I, too, have endured and risked. To those who have battled for liberty, brotherhood, and citizenship, I can say, I, too, have battled. And to those who have lived to enjoy the fruits of liberty I can say, I, too, live and rejoice. If I have pushed my example too far, I beg them to remember that I have written in part for the encouragement of a class whose aspirations need the stimulus of success."

And then he ends: "I have aimed to assure them that knowledge may be obtained under difficulties; that poverty may give place to competency; that obscurity is not an absolute bar to distinction; and that a way is open to welfare and happiness to all who will resolutely and wisely pursue that way; that neither slavery, stripes, imprisonment, nor proscription need extinguish self-respect, crush manly ambition, or paralyze effort; that no power outside of himself can prevent a man from sustaining an honorable character and a useful relation to his day and generation; that neither institutions nor friends can make a race to stand unless it has strength in its own legs; that there is no power in the world which can be relied on to help the weak against the strong, or the simple against the wise; that races, like individuals, must stand or fall by their own merits."

As has been already indicated in the course of this narrative, Frederick Douglass never formulated any definite religious creed. But no one who reads the story of his life and work can doubt that he was guided and inspired through his whole career by the highest moral and religious motives. The evidence of this is not merely his steadfast optimism and faith in the future, but in the sense in which he regarded his personal mission. From his own point of view, the work he did for his race was not merely a duty, it was a high privilege:

"Forty years of my life have been given to the cause of my people, and if I had forty years more they should all be sacredly given to the same great cause. If I have done something for that cause, I am, after all, more a debtor to it than it is a debtor to me."

Du Bois on Douglass

Herbert Aptheker

The death of Frederick Douglass in February 1895 produced a wave of public mourning among the African American community. One eulogist at a memorial service sponsored by the black Wilberforce University in Ohio was a young professor of Greek and Latin, William Edward Burghardt Du Bois. Historian Herbert Aptheker, a pioneer in black history, uncovered and republished this forgotten testament by one important race leader about his predecessor. Du Bois praised Douglass for demonstrating the extensive capabilities of the African American race to the often-prejudiced world. Du Bois especially extolled Douglass's labors as a civil rights advocate who "stood outside mere race lines and placed himself upon the broad basis of humanity."

Fresh from Fisk, Harvard and Berlin, young William Edward Burghardt Du Bois accepted an appointment as a Professor of Greek and Latin at Wilberforce University. Very soon after joining this faculty, the 27-year-old Du Bois was asked to participate in a Memorial Service to be conducted by the University on March 9, 1895. The purpose of the Service, as a one-page printed program stated, was "To Keep the Memory of Frederick Douglass," who had died in Washington, D.C. on February 20, and had been buried in Rochester, N.Y., on February 26, 1895.

The Service began with The Lord's Prayer; a scripture reading followed; music was offered at intervals. President Mitchell made introductory and Bishop Arnett concluding remarks. Others—unnamed—provided reminiscences, and Resolutions expressing sentiments appropriate to the occasion were adopted before adjournment. Three addresses were offered: Principal Jackson spoke first on "Douglass and Emancipation," a senior student, G.E. Masterson, followed

Herbert Aptheker, "Du Bois on Douglass: 1895," *Journal of Negro History*, vol. 49, October 1964, pp. 264–68. Copyright © 1964 by The Association for the Study of African American Life and History, Inc. Reproduced by permission.

on "Douglass as an Orator," and the newest faculty member discussed "Douglass as a Statesman." Professor Scarborough then delivered a Eulogy.

These proceedings were never published. The complete text, however, of the address delivered here by Du Bois has survived and is published below for the first time. The manuscript was written in pencil; it covers eleven pages, stapled together, of the type used for college examinations. The text is reproduced exactly as in the original, except that the corrections made by Du Bois are not reproduced.

The reader will observe that Du Bois' address concludes with a call to his audience to take up the torch of militancy and struggle held high for half a century by Douglass; of course, Du Bois was talking to himself, also. Two years before, in Berlin, he had entered into his diary, upon reaching his 25th birthday, the promise he then made and never forsook, ". . . to work for the rise of the Negro people . . ." In reading this speech of seventy years ago, one should remember that the year 1895 witnessed not only the death of Douglass and this oration by Du Bois; it witnessed also Booker T. Washington's Atlanta Cotton States Exposition Speech.

Speaking, then, to a Wilberforce audience, on "Douglass as a Statesman" the young Du Bois said:

Du Bois Assesses Douglass

As wanderers along an unknown path, it is due to ourselves and humanity that we pause today and seek to fathom the true meaning of the death of a long-trusted leader. We must not rush on merely crying in half-triumphant sadness "The King is dead, long live the King!" The true recognition of greatness lies not merely in well-turned phrases or memorials but in careful conscientious emulation of the life of the Dead. If we of Wilberforce desire really to appreciate Frederick Douglass we must first know what he did, and then seek in our own lives to picture forth again his wisdom his bravery and his trueness.

As an aid to this I shall say a word on one phase of his lifework, and ask during a few minutes, how far was Frederick Douglass a statesman? A statesman is the leader of a state—not necessarily an official or a diplomat, but a man who being in a position to lead, leads. Judged by this standard Douglass may be said to deserve the name. We have had many great men in the stirring half century which his active life covers, and yet amid the names of Lincoln, Seward, Garrison Sumner and Phillips, no one today hesitates to write the name of Douglass.

His whole life was given to the work of moulding public opinion toward what he firmly believed was the truth, and we can judge of his success and his wisdom only by viewing in the calm light of history some of the solutions which he offered to the great problems of our country.

First as to the slavery question: he was an abolitionist. As this is said we involuntarily say "of course." We must remember however that in those days the advocacy of the abolition of slavery was not a matter of course & that then to hundreds of trained & careful intellects any attempt to do away with slavery in this manner belonged as much to the realm of the impossible as the squaring of the circle. Men said and said with a truth and cogency we still feel today: What are you going to do with 4 millions of emancipated slaves? Either they will sink into a disgusting barbarism, or through the relentless tyranny of their ex-masters they will to all intents remain in slavery. This was a strong argument with strong supporters: yet Time has proven not to be sure that Emancipation was an untarnished good, not that these anticipated evils did not in some degree come true, but that on the whole the policy of State advocated by Douglass and his compeers was the best settlement of the problem possible at the time. Here first then he proved himself the worthy builder of a state.

On the second question in which he led public opinion, viz. the employment of black soldiers in the war we have again evidence of his foresight. The[re] is no doubt that, at the time, a vast number of people in the United States looked upon the employment of Negroes as soldiers in the same light as the[y] had previously viewed the employment of Indians in the colonial wars—viz: as an unjustifiable breach in the code of civilized warfare. Today the wisdom of the man who was perhaps chiefly instrumental in organizing the celebrated 54 & 55 Mass. regiments [during the Civil War] is as little questioned as is the bravery of those black troops and I count no little honor that flesh and blood of my own family marched in those ranks at the call of Douglass—and marched to death; but;

how can man die better
Than facing fearful odds

For the ashes of his fathers
And the temples of his gods.

On the third great question of statesmanship, men are not as unanimously agreed as to the wisdom of the course advocated by such as Douglass, and eventually carried out. I refer to the enfranchisement of the Freedmen. The civilized world looked on aghast when the United States with a stroke of the pen gave millions of degraded and ignorant men the right to be co-rulers of the nation. It was a dangerous—almost a reckless experiment, and though it has led to fewer evils than its enemies confidently expected, we must also candidly confess, it has led to dangers which its friends did not foresee. Let us bravely acknowledge today as every true man must acknowledge that for the great mass of Negro voters, the experiment of citizenship has not as yet wholly justified itself, and if we would prove the wisdom & statesmanship of our Douglass in this particular let us strive with unabating and never-ending effort to make the name of Negro citizens synonymous, not with ignorance and venality, but with honesty & intelligence.

OUR MOSES

As an advocate of civil rights Frederick Douglass stood outside mere race lines and placed himself upon the broad basis of humanity. By this he undoubtedly vastly strengthened his position in the eyes of the civilized world, in spite of any temporary weakening of it in his own land. His race has followed him largely in this respect and followed wisely. He and we have said not that all Negroes should be treated thus and so—not that all black men should be honored merely on account of their blackness, but that in the treatment which a civilized country accords its citizens, character and not color should be the sole basis of all differences. In this stand the best thought of the 19th century in all the world is with us; and as long as we keep to this broad principle—as long as we condemn lynching men, & not merely condemn lynching Negroes, so long shall we continue slowly but surely to approach the goal which this our Moses placed before us.

The first and last time I saw Douglass he lectured on Hayti and the Haytians and here again he took a position worthy of his life and reputation. It is strange that modern civilization still sanctions a code of morals between nations which if used between men would bring the severest condemnation; to steal a book is theft, but to steal an island is missionary enterprise; to tell a neighbor an untruth is to lie, but to tell a neighboring country a whole portfolio full is to be diplomatic. The whole criticism that can be brought against Douglass' Haytian ministry is that he utterly refused to be "diplomatic" and to this, we his people, say "Amen!"

I have thus briefly indicated a few of the detailed questions of state on which Frederick Douglass impressed his opinion on the nation. The greater question however underlying all is & was: What after all are the capabilities of the Negro race[?] The American people have striven to show the world that among certain peoples individuals if given a chance may rise to the highest. Douglass and his race strive to say not only may individuals of a race arise, but races in the family of nations may also rise & that too not by the horrors of war but by the battles of Peace. The preliminaries of this contention Douglass fought for us, but the main battle he has left for us. It is a stern strife where the trifler and idiot have no place but strong and fearless men, trained and experienced soldiers, will turn the tide of Battle! Can we furnish such Men & Women at Wilberforce?

The life of Douglass itself answers

"So near is grandeur to our dust
"So near is God to man
"When duty whispers low 'Thou Must'
"The Youth replies, 'I can!'"

Was Douglass a Representative Black Man?

Wilson J. Moses

In the century since Frederick Douglass's death, his historical image has become enshrined in a small pantheon of popularly recognized African American heroes, which also includes Booker T. Washington and W.E.B. Du Bois as well as more recent figures such as Martin Luther King Jr. Not every modern commentator endorses Douglass's membership in this elite group. Wilson J. Moses, the Ferree Professor of American History at Pennsylvania State University, is an author of several well-received books on nineteenth-century African American history. In an essay on Douglass excerpted here, Moses questions where Douglass truly represented the values of black Americans, in either the nineteenth or twentieth century, especially his fervent commitment to the elimination of racial distinctions. Moses credits Douglass's enduring reputation to his skills at self-promotion in white-dominated corridors of power rather than to his ability to articulate and advance the desires of most other African Americans.

Frederick Douglass may or may not have been the greatest African American abolitionist and orator of the 19th Century, but he was certainly the most accomplished master of self-projection. His autobiographical writings demonstrate the genius with which he seized and manipulated mainstream American symbols and values. By appropriating the Euro-American myth of the self-made man, Douglass guaranteed that his struggle would be canonized, not only within an African American tradition, but within the traditions of the mainstream as well. He manipulated the rhetoric of

Wilson J. Moses, "Where Honor Is Due: Frederick Douglass as Representative Black Man," *Prospects*, vol. 17, 1992, pp. 177–81, 183, 185–88. Copyright © 1992 by Cambridge University Press. Reproduced by permission.

Anglo-Saxon manhood as skillfully as did any of his white contemporaries, including such master manipulators as Abraham Lincoln, Ralph Waldo Emerson, and Phineas T. Barnum. I mention Douglass along with these wily exemplars of American showmanship, not because I want to drag out embarrassing cliches about making heroes more human, but in order to address the truly monumental nature of Douglass's accomplishments. Douglass, like Lincoln, Emerson, and Barnum, was abundantly endowed with the spiderish craft and foxlike cunning that are often marks of self-made men.

Douglass, like his bluff contemporary Walt Whitman, made his living by the art of self-celebration, a skill that has always figured in the strategies of American literary figures. He sang his song of himself, through four main versions of his autobiography, creating himself as a mythic figure and racial icon. The result is that even scholars and historians who may be relatively unfamiliar with other black American personalities of the 19th Century are acquainted with the major events of Douglass's life, or at least with his version of them. He was born into slavery in 1818, escaped to the North in 1838 and, with amazing rapidity, by 1840 was well on the way to establishing himself as the principal black abolitionist in the United States. Among his other accomplishments, Douglass served as a newspaper editor, Civil War recruiter, president of the Freedman's Bank, minister to Haiti, recorder of deeds, and Marshall of the District of Columbia. In the final analysis, he was a man of great dignity, principle, and courage, but he was also a showman, and he made his living mainly by cultivating the myth of Frederick Douglass.

When he attempted to function as a businessman or politician, he sometimes waded in beyond his depth, and thus he was embarrassed by the failure of the Freedman's Bank, shortly after he assumed its presidency. His tenure as minister to Haiti was troubled from the beginning. . . .

DOUGLASS MOLDS HIS HISTORICAL IMAGE

But even Douglass's setbacks were somehow transmuted into victories by the alchemy of a brilliant personality and the fact that black America has always had a desperate need for heroes. Nonetheless, it must be admitted that many aspects of Douglass's life and writings are controversial. No se-

rious historian can ignore the problem of self-serving selec-
tivity that lies behind the veil of homely modesty that he as-
sumes in his autobiographical writings. The task of every biographer of Frederick Douglass has been to fill in some of
the discreet omissions in Douglass's skillful work of self-
promotion. Historians and literary scholars are increasingly
aware of the craft with which Douglass manipulated audiences and readers, and they have recently provided us with
considerable information that Douglass did not see fit to reveal. Many of these matters were discussed in the first full-
length biography of Douglass, published by Benjamin Quarles in 1948. More recent biographers have built on Quarles's
work, giving us a portrait that is admirable and believable;
nonetheless, in far too many instances, Douglass has been
allowed to dictate the terms of his own biography.

Because even the best biographies of Douglass have been
appendices to his own brilliant autobiographical writings,
the point is often forgotten that Douglass was not a gigantic
abnormality in black American history, but in many ways a
typical black American man of the class and region he represented. In typical American fashion, Douglass sought in
his writings to demonstrate his individuality, along with his
individualism. The very self-reliance and independence that
he stressed in his autobiographies represented conformity to
the American type of the self-made man. Thus, Douglass
was, to use Emerson's phrase, a representative man. Much
of the present-day biographical and literary treatment of
Douglass makes him appear to be exceptional. For his own
part, Douglass at times stressed the Emersonian dictum that
the great man is often great because he is representative, not
because he is exceptional. Self-reliance, for him as for Emerson, often existed in the paradox of blending one's ego into
larger "transcendental" forces, of believing that what is true
of one's self is true of others. Douglass's concept of self-
reliance, like Emerson's, was grounded in the principle of
universality rather than difference. Douglass was, as I hope
to show presently, not only a representative man, but a representative *black* man.

On the other hand, there were ways in which he was not
representative. Douglass seemed, at times, to be less attuned
to the cultural sentiments of black Americans and to their political struggles than were some other black men among his
contemporaries. Among black-power advocates, he is cele-

brated as a prophet of self-determination. They celebrate his founding of *The North Star*, an independent newspaper, and it is with relish that they recall his rallying cry "We must be our own representatives!" But Douglass could change positions dramatically on black-power-related issues. He did at times champion black institutions, and then on other occasions he denounced them as self-segregating. Douglass's ideology was thoroughly inconsistent, usually opportunistic, and always self-serving. I suspect that if Douglass were alive today, he would be as uncontrollable as ever, and that his often shifting ideology would be now, as it was then, often unacceptable to liberals and conservatives alike. . . .

DOUGLASS AND WOMEN

A case in point is Douglass's relationship to the women's movement. He did indeed commendably support women's suffrage, but this support was at times less than lukewarm. Douglass gave black male suffrage a much higher priority than white female suffrage, even when his feminist friends became exasperated with him. While on the one hand he got along well with white liberal women, and even married one of them, he was not afraid to confront them when he felt their interests to be in conflict with his as a black male.

Today there is endless discussion of Douglass's private life and his friendships with women, both black and white, for we now know much more about his personal affairs than did his earlier biographers. Douglass had a commanding personality; he was strikingly handsome and stood over six feet tall; he was athletic and he possessed an intense sexual attractiveness. I believe that a great deal of what he accomplished was a result of his magnetic virility. . . .

In recent years, black feminists have become increasingly critical of Douglass's treatment of his first wife. Anna Douglass was a dutiful helpmate to her husband; she was a hard worker and a thrifty housewife. A portion of Douglass's financial success has been attributed to her able administration of his domestic finances, but she was not up to the management of a newspaper and she apparently never learned to read. Furthermore, it does not seem that she provided Douglass with much in the way of intellectual companionship; for this, he often went outside his home. The women were usually white, and his friendship in later years with the young journalist Ida B. Wells is the best known intellectual friendship he is known to have developed with a black woman. . . .

Douglass's ambivalent feelings toward Sojourner Truth are seldom discussed. Sojourner was a dynamic Black woman abolitionist who once caused him public annoyance by responding to his declamations with the question, "Frederick, is God dead?" This was a matter of some embarrassment, since Douglass was more than once plagued by charges of irreligiosity. Sojourner Truth, on the other hand, was closely associated with the strident religiosity of the day and was much more closely related to proletarian evangelical Christianity than was the transcendental Douglass, with his increasing pretensions to gentility.

It is not difficult to understand why Douglass played up to white feminists after the demise of the abolitionist movement, for in them he found a receptive audience for his writings and speeches. Within this view, his marriage to a white feminist was not only an affair of the heart, but a significant political move. Black men and women were not well positioned to help him maintain public visibility once the abolitionist movement had run its course; the women's rights movement, headed by white women, still offered him a forum. Another way of seeing it was that in his first marriage he made an alliance with a free black woman who could assist him in his flight to freedom, whereas in his second marriage he cemented ties with his new audience, which was largely composed of white feminists. . . .

RELATIONSHIPS WITH OTHER BLACK LEADERS

In a chapter of his autobiography of 1892 entitled "Honor to whom Honor Is Due," Douglass acknowledged several black men who were rivals and who clearly possessed intellects and rhetorical skills of their own. Douglass, to his credit, did pay tribute to Samuel Ringgold Ward, whom he acknowledged as the greatest black orator of the day. Ward probably had a hand in persuading Douglass away from the sterile and narrow Garrisonian interpretation of the Constitution, since it was during a debate with Ward that Douglass was forced to analyze the logic of the Garrisonian position. Ward presented him with the position putatively held by the majority of black people—that the Constitution could bear interpretation as an antislavery document. . . .

Douglass's relationship with Martin Delany was also significant. When in 1848, over the objections of Garrison,

Douglass founded his newspaper, *The North Star*, it was with Delany as coeditor, but Douglass soon fell out with Delany over a number of issues, most important among them being the issue of black pride. "I thank God for making me a man simply," said Douglass, "but Delany always thanks him for making him a '*black* man.'" Douglass considered Delany a racial chauvinist and an extremist. Delany did in fact show a great interest in Africa and in the prospects of founding a national homeland for the black race, a position that Douglass could not endorse. He once said that, if he were inclined to go to Africa, he would unhesitatingly enroll under Delany's leadership, but Douglass had no interest either in going or in supporting the movement. . . .

Frederick Douglass

Douglass's hostility to the black congressman John Mercer Langston is one of the more intriguing puzzles in the lives of the two men. Their backgrounds as favored slaves of mixed background were similar, but similarity of background does not necessarily provide a basis for political friendships. In 1850, when Douglass was thirty-three and Langston twenty-one, the two had traveled together on an Eastern speaking tour. But, by 1853, Langston was accusing Douglass of using his newspaper primarily as a means of self-promotion. The journal reported the most trivial of events in the East, he wrote, but "Men of the West cannot be noticed . . . [*T*]*he North Star*, edited by Frederick Douglass, is not the organ of the colored people." A not altogether friendly rivalry persisted for many years. . . .

We seldom hear of Douglass's sometimes uneasy relationship with Alexander Crummell (1819–98), the American-born and educated son of a West African captive, and prominent spokesman of the back-to-Africa movement. Douglass had accused Crummell of abandonment during the 1850s at a time when he himself was being accused of dereliction by the nationalist emigrationists. Crummell, after several years' residence in England attending Cambridge University and lecturing for the abolitionist cause, had migrated to Liberia, West Africa, and dedicated himself to the building of a black republic. In 1855, Douglass called on him in the name of black unity to renounce the "agreeable duty" that anyone could perform, and to return to the United States to perform the "disagreeable duty" of abolitionist struggle. This spirit of accusation was consistent in the writings of Douglass when addressing Crummell, . . . Delany, and other black nationalists. Douglass maintained his confrontational stance long after the constitutional abolition of slavery and the decline of nationalist versus abolitionist controversy. In 1885, he challenged the position that Crummell took during a speech at Storer College, where Crummell had argued that black American leaders must stop dwelling on slavery and focus their attention on "new ideas and new aims for a new era." Douglass vociferously objected, saying that we should forever hold slavery in mind. Douglass and Crummell also disagreed over the need for black social institutions. Douglass considered them harmful, while Crummell insisted that they would remain a necessity of life for many years to come. . . .

DOUGLASS THE TOTAL ASSIMILATIONIST

I do not believe that it is Douglass's fault that in the final analysis his status was giganticized until he came to be seen as the only great black man of the 19th Century. Part of the reason is that many of Douglass's rivals were too black, and there has been a tendency to downplay the significance of 19th-Century black-power advocates in favor of the integrationist, assimilationist Douglass. . . .

Intermarriage and race mixing have never been among the spiritual strivings of the majority of African Americans, but for Douglass racial amalgamation was the ultimate goal. He was thus, in at least one respect, not a representative man. Moreover, he was not a race man, for although he remained true to the goal of racial equality in America, he repudiated any special feelings of racial pride, saying,

> Our color is the gift of the Almighty. We should neither be proud of it nor ashamed of it. . . . I have seen myself charged with a lack of race pride. I am not ashamed of that charge. I have no apology or vindication to offer. If fifty years of uncompromising devotion to the cause of the colored man in this country does not vindicate me, I am content to live without vindication. . . . When a colored man is charged with a want of race pride, he may well ask, What race? for a large

percentage of the colored race are related in some degree to more than one race. But the whole assumption of race pride is ridiculous.

The historian William McFeely and the conservative columnist George Will have praised Frederick Douglass for his repudiation of reverse racism. Are we to assume then that Americans, black or white, have come to endorse Douglass's advocacy of a "color blind society" based on the biological amalgamation and cultural absorption of African Americans? That was the message of Frederick Douglass, but does this embody the spirit of black America? What does it mean to be a hero? What does it mean to have the shaggy-headed leonine portrait of Frederick Douglass staring down at us from the bulletin boards of schoolrooms across America during Black History Month?

My answer to the first question is that black Americans have always rejected Douglass's vision of America, and that neither black nor white Americans are committed to the eradication of racial distinctions in American life. While the spirit of black folk in the United States is clearly democratic and egalitarian, it is also essentially one of racial self-determination and ethnic pride. Douglass believed that the concept of ethnic pride and black unity was a mistake. He felt that it was actually unsafe for black people to stand together as a separate entity. We should beware the danger of isolating ourselves. We should not attempt to be "a nation within a nation." Rightly or wrongly, the spirit of black folk runs counter to such talk. There may be some exceptions, but these are rare and remarkable. The essential separatism of the black American people is to be seen in its marriage patterns. Marriage outside the race is uncommon and will probably continue to be so for the foreseeable future. Douglass ultimately renounced not only marital separatism, but all forms of racial unity and ethnic pride. Douglass offered the example of his own social adjustment, not only as a statement of personal preference, but as a proposed solution to the race problem in America.

JUDGING DOUGLASS

If Frederick Douglass represents the spirit of black folk, then, he certainly represents it in all of its complexities, ambivalences, and contradictions. Who is to say whether the genius of self-promotion that characterized Douglass was more attributable to African American exuberance or to a typically American showmanship and flimflammery? Like many black leaders of the present day, and many American leaders throughout our history, Douglass made an industry of himself. When compared with other black men of the 19th Century, Douglass was in no way a giant among dwarfs, but certainly he managed to stamp his name on an era much more effectively than did Martin Delany or John Mercer Langston. And the great irony of Douglass's sainthood is that he openly violated some of the most sacred canons of African American political culture. At the peak of his power and influence, Douglass scoffed at the idea of black unity, opposed the idea of separate black institutions, and sometimes denied the need for any concept of racial pride. And yet he continued to participate in black institutions, took pride in black accomplishments, and exploited his status as a black spokesman.

Since Douglass seems to have attained an unassailable position in the pantheon of heroes we dutifully trot out every year for black history month, it is appropiate for us to ask what we really mean when we speak of an African American hero. Academic politicians will never find it necessary to ask the question, of course; for them it will be adequate simply to say that black people need heroes. After all, doesn't everyone need heroes? Hero worshippers are seldom committed to accurate reporting of what great men and women have thought and said. Analytical reflection on their writings is neither desired nor tolerated. Hero worshippers are looking for paper dolls that they can call their own, pasteboard silhouettes who can be clothed in the ideological garb of passing fancies.

Perhaps much of the continuing popularity of Frederick Douglass may be attributed to the facility with which he can be adapted to the conveniences of any hour. Douglass's aphoristic pontifications may be conveniently invoked on almost every occasion in this age of the "sound bite," and his ideologically malleable pronouncements may be rationalized with Emersonian blandness, as we recall the facile observation that "Consistency is the hobgoblin of small minds." Douglass may be claimed by nationalists like Molefi K. Asante as a symbol of militant black messianism or by George Will as a representative of some vaguely imagined and yet-to-be-glimpsed color-blind society. Perhaps one reason for our continuing fascination with Douglass is the amorphous quality of his symbolism. He seems to encompass the continuing ambivalence of black men in America with respect to many issues, including separatism, integration, Afrocentrism, Eurocentrism, and male-female relationships. He is, perhaps, a more representative black man than even he realized, and perhaps more typical than he suspected of those other 19th-Century black men to whom he paid cursory and fleeting tribute in his autobiographical writings.

APPENDIX OF DOCUMENTS

DOCUMENT 1: SELF-EMANCIPATION

In his 1845 autobiography, Douglass described a brutal fight that he had had a decade earlier with the Maryland "slave breaker," Edward Covey. Douglass's master had charged Covey with making the teen-aged slave more compliant. Douglass recalls his victory in this battle as the beginning of his psychological emancipation from slavery.

Long before daylight, I was called to go and rub, curry, and feed the horses. I obeyed, and was glad to obey. But whilst thus engaged, whilst in the act of throwing down some blades from the loft, Mr. Covey entered the stable with a long rope; and just as I was half out of the loft, he caught hold of my legs, and was about tying me. As soon as I found what he was up to, I gave a sudden spring, and as I did so, he holding to my legs, I was brought sprawling on the stable floor. Mr. Covey seemed now to think he had me, and could do what he pleased; but at this moment—from whence came the spirit I don't know—I resolved to fight; and, suiting my action to the resolution, I seized Covey hard by the throat; and as I did so, I rose. He held on to me, and I to him. My resistance was so entirely unexpected, that Covey seemed taken all aback. He trembled like a leaf. This gave me assurance, and I held him uneasy, causing the blood to run where I touched him with the ends of my fingers. . . .

He asked me if I meant to persist in my resistance. I told him I did, come what might; that he had used me like a brute for six months, and that I was determined to be used so no longer. With that, he strove to drag me to a stick that was lying just out of the stable door. He meant to knock me down. But just as he was leaning over to get the stick, I seized him with both hands by his collar, and brought him by a sudden snatch to the ground. . . .

We were at it for nearly two hours. Covey at length let me go, puffing and blowing at a great rate, saying that if I had not resisted, he would not have whipped me half so much. The truth was, that he had not whipped me at all. I considered him as getting entirely the worst end of the bargain; for he had drawn no blood from me, but I had from him. The whole six months afterwards, that I spent with Mr. Covey, he never laid the weight of his finger upon me in anger. He would occasionally say, he didn't want to get hold of me again. "No," thought I, "you need not; for you will come off worse than you did before."

This battle with Mr. Covey was the turning-point in my career as a slave. It rekindled the few expiring embers of freedom, and revived within me a sense of my own manhood. It recalled the departed self-confidence, and inspired me again with a determination to be free. The gratification afforded by the triumph was a full compensation for whatever else might follow, even death itself. He only can understand the deep satisfaction which I experienced, who has himself repelled by force the bloody arm of slavery. I felt as I never felt before. It was a glorious resurrection, from the tomb of slavery, to the heaven of freedom. My long-crushed spirit rose, cowardice departed, bold defiance took its place; and I now resolved that, however long I might remain a slave in form, the day had passed forever when I could be a slave in fact. I did not hesitate to let it be known of me, that the white man who expected to succeed in whipping, must also succeed in killing me.

Frederick Douglass, *Narrative of the Life of Frederick Douglass, an American Slave.* Boston: Anti-Slavery Office, 1845.

DOCUMENT 2: DOUGLASS AS PREACHER

Early in his life, both in Maryland and Massachusetts, Douglass had served as a lay preacher in congregations of the small African Methodist Episcopal Zion Church. In correspondence many years later, he recalled the formative impact of that religious work on his later career as an abolitionist and civil rights leader. Douglass remembered his time preaching as "among the happiest days of my life."

My connection with the African Methodist Episcopal Zion Church began in 1838. This was soon after my escape from slavery and my arrival in New Bedford. Before leaving Maryland I was a member of the Methodist Church in Dallas Street, Baltimore, and should have joined a branch of that Church in New Bedford, Mass., had I not discovered the spirit of prejudice and the unholy connection of that Church with slavery. Hence I joined a little branch of Zion, of which Rev. William Serrington was the minister. I found him a man of deep piety, and of high intelligence. His character attracted me, and I received from him much excellent advice and brotherly sympathy. When he was removed to another station Bishop Rush sent us a very different man, in the person of Rev. Peter Ross, a man of high character, but of very little education. After him came Rev. Thomas James. I was deeply interested not only in these ministers, but also in Revs. Jehill Beman, Dempsy Kennedy, John P. Thompson, and Leven Smith, all of whom visited and preached in the little schoolhouse on Second Street, New Bedford, while I resided there. My acquaintance with Bishop Rush was also formed while I was in New Bedford.

It is impossible for me to tell how far my connection with these devoted men influenced my career. As early as 1839 I obtained a licence from the Quarterly Conference as a local preacher, and often occupied the pulpit by request of the preacher in charge. No doubt that the exercise of my gifts in this vocation, and my association with the excellent men to whom I have referred, helped to prepare me for the wider sphere of usefulness which I have since occupied. It was from this Zion church that I went forth to the work of delivering my brethren from bondage, and this new vocation, which separated me from New Bedford and finally so enlarged my views of duty, separated me also from the calling of a local preacher. My connection with the little church continued long after I was in the antislavery field. I look back to the days I spent in little Zion, New Bedford, in the several capacities of sexton, steward, class leader, clerk, and local preacher, as among the happiest days of my life.

Lenwood G. Davis, "Frederick Douglass as a Preacher, and One of His Last Most Significant Letters (in Documents)," *Journal of Negro History*, Summer 1981.

DOCUMENT 3: THE SLAVERY OF ALCOHOL

While traveling in the British Isles, Douglass was called upon to address many diverse audiences. In 1846, he was asked to speak to a temperance convention in Paisley, Scotland. He used the opportunity to compare the evils of alcohol consumption to slave owning.

I have been excluded from the temperance movement in the United States, because God has given me a skin not colored like yours. I can speak, however, in regard to the facts concerning ardent spirits, for the same spirit which makes a white man makes a black man drunk too. Indeed, in this I can find proof of my identity with the family of man. The colored man in the United States has great difficulties in the way of his moral, social, and religious advancement. Almost every step he takes toward mental, moral, or social improvement is repulsed by the cold indifference or the active mob of the white. He is compelled to live an outcast from society; he is as it were, a border or selvage on the great cloth of humanity, and the very fact of his degradation is given as a reason why he should be continued in the condition of a slave. The blacks are to a considerable extent intemperate and of course vicious in other respects and this is counted against them as a reason why their emancipation from intemperance, because I believe it would be the means—a great and glorious means—towards helping to break their physical chains, and letting them go free. . . .

I have had some experience of intemperance as well as of slavery. In the Southern States, masters induce their slaves to drink whisky, in order to keep them from devising ways and means by which to obtain their freedom. In order to make a man a slave, it is necessary to silence or drown his mind. It is not the flesh that objects to being bound—it is the spirit. It is not the mere animal part—it is the immortal mind which distinguishes man from the brute creation. To blind his affections, it is necessary to bedim and bedizzy his understanding. In no other way can this be so well accomplished as using ardent spirits. . . .

I am a temperance man because I am an anti-slavery man; and I am an anti-slavery man because I love my fellow men. There is no other cure for intemperance but total abstinence. Will not temperance do, says one? No. Temperance was tried in America, but it would not do. The total abstinence principle came and made clean work of it. It is now seen spreading its balmy influence over the whole of that land. It is seen in making peace where there was war. It has planted light and education where there was nothing but degradation, and darkness, and misery. It is your duty to plant—you cannot do all, but if you plant, God has promised, and will give the increase.

Philip S. Foner, ed. *The Life and Writings of Frederick Douglass*, 5 vols. New York: International Publishers, 1950–1975.

DOCUMENT 4: DEAR MASTER

In December 1847, Douglass began to edit and publish his own anti-slavery newspaper, the North Star, *in Rochester, New York. The following September, he used his editorial columns to address a public letter to his former Maryland master, Thomas Auld. Douglass lectured Auld about his current as well as past mistreatment of his slaves as a means of exposing the cruel nature of slavery to all of his readers.*

The responsibility which you have assumed . . . [as a slave master] is truly awful—and how you could stagger under it these many years is marvellous. Your mind must have become darkened, your heart hardened, your conscience seared and petrified, or you would have long since thrown off the accursed load and sought relief at the hands of a sin forgiving God. How, let me ask, would you look upon me, were I some dark night in company with a band of hardened villains, to enter the precincts of your own elegant dwelling and seize the person of your own lovely daughter Amanda, and carry her off from your family, friends and all the loved ones of her youth—make her my slave—compel her to work, and I take her wages—place her name on my ledger as property—disregard her personal rights—fetter the powers of her immortal soul by denying her the right and privilege of learning to read and write—feed her coarsely—clothe her scantily, and whip her on the naked back occasionally; more and still more horrible, leave her unprotected—a degraded victim to the brutal lust of fiendish overseers who would pollute, blight, and blast her fair soul—rob her of all dignity—destroy her virtue, and annihilate all in her person the graces that adorn the character of virtuous womanhood? I ask how would you regard me, if such were my conduct? Oh! the vocabulary of the damned would not afford a word suf[fi]ciently infernal, to express your idea of my God-provoking wickedness. Yet sir, your treatment of my beloved sisters is in all essential points, precisely like the case I have now supposed. Damning as would be such a deed on my part, it would be no more so than that which you have committed against me and my sisters.

I will now bring this letter to a close, you shall hear from me again unless you let me hear from you. I intend to make use of you as a weapon with which to assail the system of slavery—as a means of concentrating public attention on the system, and deepening their horror of trafficking in the souls and bodies of men. I shall make use of you as a means of exposing the character of the American church and clergy—and as a means of bringing this guilty nation with yourself to repentance. In doing this I entertain no malice towards you personally. There is no roof under which you would be more safe than mine, and there is nothing in my house which you might need for your comfort, which I would not readily grant. Indeed, I should esteem it a privilege, to set you an example as to how mankind ought to treat each other.

Frederick Douglass, editorial, *North Star*, September 8, 1848.

DOCUMENT 5: OPPOSITION TO AFRICAN COLONIZATION

Following the passage of the Fugitive Slave Law of 1850, efforts to persuade free blacks to emigrate from the United States to such places as Africa or the Caribbean increased substantially. In an 1851 speech in Buffalo, Douglass argued that by virtue of their many years of hard toil African Americans had earned the right to remain in the United States.

Sir, the slaveholders have long been anxious to get rid of the free colored person of this country. They know that where we are left free, blacks though we are, thick-skulled as they call us, we shall become intelligent, and, moreover, that as we become intelligent, in just that proportion shall we become an annoyance to them in their slaveholding. They are anxious therefore to get us out of the country. They know that a hundred thousand intelligent, upright, industrious and persevering black men in the northern states must command respect and sympathy, must encircle themselves with the regard of a large class of the virtue-loving, industry-loving people of the north, and that whatever sympathy, whatever respect they are able to command must have a reflex influence upon slavery. And, therefore, they say "*out with them,*" let us get rid of them!

For my part, I am not disposed to leave, and, I think, our friend must have been struck with the singular kind of applause at certain sayings of his, during the address—an applause that seemed to come from the galleries, from the door, and from that part of the house that does not wish to be mixed up with the platform. Straws show which way the wind blows (applause). I fancied, too, that when our friend was portraying the blessings that would result from our removal from this land to Jamaica, that delightful visions were floating before the minds of those gentlemen in the distance. (Great applause.)

Now sir, I want to say on behalf of any negroes I have the honor to represent, that we *have* been with, still *are* with you, and *mean* to be with you *to the end.* (Cheers.) It may seem ungrateful, but there are some of us who are resolved that you shall not get rid of your colored relations. (Immense applause.). . .

But how stands the matter? I believe that simultaneously with the landing of the pilgrims, there landed slaves on the shores of this continent, and that for two hundred and thirty years and more we have had a foothold on this continent. We have grown up with you, we have watered your soil with our tears, nourished it with our blood, tilled it with our hard hands. Why should we not stay here? We came when it was a wilderness, and were the pioneers of civilization on this continent. *We* levelled your forests, *our hands* removed the stumps from your fields, and raised the first crops and brought the first produce to your tables. We have been with you, are still with you, have been with you in adversity, and by the help of God will be with you in prosperity. (Repeated applause.)

Frederick Douglass, transcript of 1851 speech, *Frederick Douglass' Paper*, October 2, 1851.

DOCUMENT 6: MEANING OF THE FOURTH OF JULY

In 1852, Douglass delivered one of his best-remembered abolitionist speeches to a packed hall in Rochester, New York. He assailed the hypocrisy of the typical Fourth of July orators who turned a blind eye to the existence of slavery in the so-called land of liberty.

Fellow-citizens, pardon me, allow me to ask, why am I called upon to speak here to-day? What have I, or those I represent, to do with your national independence? Are the great principles of political freedom and of natural justice, embodied in that Declaration of Independence, extended to us? And am I, therefore, called upon to bring our humble offering to the national altar, and to confess the benefits and express devout gratitude for the blessings resulting from your independence to us?

Would to God, both for your sakes and ours, that an affirmative answer could be truthfully returned to these questions! Then would my task be light, and my burden easy and delightful. For *who* is there so cold, that a nation's sympathy could not warm him? Who so obdurate and dead to the claims of gratitude, that would not thankfully acknowledge such priceless benefits? Who so stolid and selfish, that would not give his voice to swell the hallelujahs of a nation's jubilee, when the chains of servitude had been torn from his limbs? I am not that man. In a case like that, the dumb might eloquently speak, and the "lame man leap as an hart."

But, such is not the state of the cast. I say it with a sad sense of the disparity between us. I am not included within the pale of this glorious anniversary! Your high independence only reveals the immeasurable distance between us. The blessings in which you, this day, rejoice, are not enjoyed in common. The rich inheritance of justice, liberty, prosperity and independence, bequeathed by your fathers, is shared by you, not by me. The sunlight that brought life and healing to you, has brought stripes and death to me. This Fourth [of] July is *yours*, not *mine. You* may rejoice, *I* must mourn. To drag a man in fetters into the grand illuminated temple of liberty, and call upon him to join you in joyous anthems, were inhuman mockery and sacrilegious irony. Do you mean, citizens, to mock me, by asking me to speak to-day? If so, there is a parallel to your conduct. And let me warn you that it is dangerous to copy the example of a nation whose crimes, towering up to heaven, were thrown down by the breath of the Almighty, burying that nation in irrecoverable ruin! I can to-day take up the plaintive lament of a peeled and woe-smitten people! . . .

What, to the American slave, is your 4th of July? I answer: a day that reveals to him, more than all other days in the year, the gross injustice and cruelty to which he is the constant victim. To him, your celebration is a sham; your boasted liberty, an unholy license; your national greatness, swelling vanity; your sounds of rejoicing are empty and heartless; your denunciations of tyrants, brass fronted impudence; your shouts of liberty and equality, hollow mockery; your prayers and hymns, your sermons and thanksgivings, with all your religious parade, and solemnity, are, to him, mere bombast, fraud, deception, impiety, and hypocrisy—a thin veil to cover up crimes which would disgrace a nation of savages. There is not a nation on the earth guilty of practices, more shocking and bloody, than are the people of these United States, at this very hour.

Go where you may, search where you will, roam through all the monarchies and despotisms of the old world, travel through South America, search out every abuse, and when you have found the last, lay your facts by the side of the everyday practices of this nation, and you will say with me, that, for revolting barbarity and shameless hypocrisy, America reigns without a rival.

Frederick Douglass, *"What to the Slave Is the Fourth of July?": An Oration, delivered in Corinthian Hall, Rochester, July 5th, 1852.* Rochester, NY: Lee, Mann & Co., 1852.

DOCUMENT 7: ALL RACES ARE EQUAL

In the 1850s, defenders of slavery attempted to use scientific evidence to prove the inherent inferiority of the Negro race as a means of defending the institution of slavery from abolitionist criticism. In a well-researched speech delivered at the Western Reserve College in

Ohio, Douglass used both logical and scientific arguments to rebut such claims.

To know whether [a] negro is a man, it must first be known what constitutes a man. Here, as well as elsewhere, I take it, that the "coat must be cut according to the cloth." It is not necessary, in order to establish the manhood of any one making the claim, to prove that such an one equals Clay in eloquence, or Webster and Calhoun in logical force and directness; for, tried by such standards of mental power as these, it is apprehended that very few could claim the high designation of *man*. Yet something like this folly is seen in the arguments directed against the humanity of the negro. His faculties and powers, uneducated and unimproved, have been contrasted with those of the highest cultivation; and the world has then been called upon to behold the immense and amazing difference between the man admitted, and the man disputed. The fact that these intellects, so powerful and so controlling, are almost, if not quite, as exceptional to the general rule of humanity in one direction, as the specimen negroes are in the other, is quite overlooked.

Man is distinguished from all other animals, by the possession of certain definite faculties and powers, as well as by physical organization and proportions. He is the only two-handed animal on the earth—the only one that laughs, and nearly the only one that weeps. Men instinctively distinguish between men and brutes. Common sense itself is scarcely needed to detect the absence of manhood in a monkey, or to recognize its presence in a negro. His speech, his reason, his power to acquire and to retain knowledge, his heaven-erected face, his habitudes, his hopes, his fears, his aspirations, his prophecies, plant between him and the brute creation, a distinction as eternal as it is palpable. Away, therefore, with all the scientific moonshine that would connect men with monkeys; that would have the world believe that humanity, instead of resting on its own characteristic pedestal—gloriously independent—is a sort of sliding scale, making one extreme brother to the ou-rang-ou-tang, and the other to angels, and all the rest intermediates! Tried by all the usual, and all the *un*usual tests, whether mental, moral, physical, or psychological, the negro is a MAN—considering him as possessing knowledge, or needing knowledge, his elevation or his degradation, his virtues, or his vices—whichever road you take, you reach the same conclusion, the negro is a MAN. His good and his bad, his innocence and his guilt, his joys and his sorrows, proclaim his manhood in speech that all mankind practically and readily understand[s].

Frederick Douglass, *"The Claims of the Negro Ethnologically Considered": An Address Before the Literary Societies of Western Reserve College, at Commencement, July 12, 1854.* Rochester, NY: Lee, Mann & Co., 1854.

DOCUMENT 8: SLAVERY ABOLISHED IN THE WEST INDIES

In 1834, the British Parliament abolished slavery in its West Indian colonies. Thereafter until the start of the American Civil War, abolitionists celebrated the anniversary of this event every August 1, by sponsoring parades, concerts, and orations. In an 1858 speech at such a commemoration, Douglass defended the achievements of the emancipated West Indian blacks against criticism from slavery apologists.

One word as to the propriety of calling West India Emancipation an experiment. I object to it. I take it that this is one of the tricks of Slavery, and is of a piece with the character of that fraudulent business. There is obviously no more reason for calling West India Emancipation an experiment than for calling the law of gravitation an experiment. Liberty is not a device or an experiment, but a law of nature dating back to man's creation, and if this fundamental law is a failure, the responsibility is not with the British Parliament, not with the British people, but with the great Author of this law. Slavery is the experiment in this case. God made man upright, but man has sought out many inventions, and Slavery is one of them. It is an experiment by which men seek to live without labor, to eat bread by the sweat of another man's brow, to get gold without digging it, and to become rich without using one's own faculties and powers to obtain riches. This is the real experiment.

But in answer to the charge that West Indian Emancipation is a failure, I frankly admit that in some respects it has failed. It has failed to keep Slavery in the West Indies under the name of Liberty. It has failed to change the name without changing the character of the thing. The negroes have really been emancipated, and are no longer slaves. Herein is the real failure. Emancipation has failed to keep negroes out of civil office, it has failed to keep them out of the jury box, off the judge's bench, and out of the Colonial Legislature, for colored men have risen to all these stations since Emancipation. It has failed to keep the lands of Jamaica in the hands of the few and out of the hands of the many. It has failed to make men work for a planter at small wages, when they can work for themselves for larger wages. In a word, West Indian Emancipation has failed just as putting new wine into old bottles or sewing new cloth upon an old garment, will fail. The failure is not with the new, but with the old—not with the present, but with the past. Plain enough it is, to common sense and common reflection, that liberty cannot prosper upon the old conditions and with and by the old methods and machinery, which are adapted to a state of Slavery. The old plantation system of the Southern States of the American Union, grow out of, and are adapted to Slavery. They belong to feudal ages, and to feudal circumstances, where the land and the people are alike owned by a few lordly proprietors. In such circumstances, where the toiling masses are all sacrificed to a limited and privileged class of slaveholders, it is easy to keep up great establishments and flourishing estates. The explanation of the failure of West India emancipation will become very clear if these facts are kept in mind.

Frederick Douglass, transcript of 1858 speech, *Frederick Douglass' Paper*, August 12, 1858.

DOCUMENT 9: BLACK MEN ENLIST

Following the issuance of the Emancipation Proclamation, the Union began enlisting blacks for its army in the Civil War. Soon after, Douglass began recruiting black soldiers to serve in two all-black infantry regiments being raised by the state of Massachusetts. Douglass made enlistment speeches all across the North such as the following one given in New York City in February 1863.

Do you ask me whether black men will freely enlist in the service of the country? I tell you that that depends upon the white men of the country. The Government must assure them of protection as soldiers, and give them a fair chance of winning distinction and glory in common with other soldiers. (Cheers.) They must not be made the mere hewers of wood and drawers of water for the army. When a man leaves home, family, and security, to risk his limbs and life in the field of battle, for God's sake let him have all the honor which he may achieve, let his color be what it may. If, by the fortunes of war he is flung into the hands of the Rebels, let him be assured that the loyal Government will not desert him, but will hold the Confederate Government strictly responsible, as much for a black as for a white soldier. (Applause.) Give us fair play, and open here your recruiting offices, and their doors shall be crowded with black recruits to fight the battles of the country. (Loud cheers.) Do your part, my white fellow-countrymen, and we will do ours. . . .

I know the colored men of the North; I know the colored men of the South. They are ready to rally under the stars and stripes at the first tap of the drum. Give them a chance; stop calling them "niggers," and call them soldiers. (Applause.) Give them a chance to seek the bauble [bubble] reputation at the cannon's mouth. Stop telling them they can't fight, and tell them they can fight and shall fight, and they will fight, and fight with vengeance. Give them a chance. The most delicate lady in the city of New York can ride by the side of a black man, if he is there as a servant. Even the most fastidious of our Generals can be waited on by colored men. Why should they object to our fighting? We were with you on the banks of the Mobile, good enough to fight with you under Gen. Jackson. Why not let us fight by your side under Gen. Hooker? (Loud cheering.) We shall have a chance yet, and I tell you to whom I am looking for this. I have great faith, as I told you more than a year ago, in the virtue of the people of the North; I have more in the persistent villainy of the South. (Laughter and applause.) I tell you that under their tent we shall yet be able to accept the aid of the colored man. Away with prejudice, away with folly, and in this death struggle for liberty, country, and permanent security, let the black, iron hand of the colored man fall heavily on the head of the slaveholding traitors and rebels and lay them low. Give them a chance! Give them a chance. I don't say they are great fighters. I don't say they will fight better than other men. All I say is, give them a chance.

Frederick Douglass, transcript of 1863 speech, *Douglass' Monthly*, March 1863.

DOCUMENT 10: THE BLACK MAN'S RIGHT TO VOTE

Even following emancipation, many states balked at granting the ballot to the recently emancipated slave. Former abolitionists and the new freedmen placed pressure on Congress to enact a constitutional amendment to make black male suffrage the national policy. In 1866, Douglass addressed the following plea to Congress for such action.

A very limited statement of the argument for impartial suffrage, and for including the negro in the body politic, would require more space than can be reasonably asked here. It is supported by reasons as broad as the nature of man, and as numerous as the wants of society. Man is the only government-making animal in the world. His right to a participation in the production and operation of government is an inference from his nature, as direct and self-evident as is his right to acquire property or education. It is no less a crime against the manhood of a man, to declare that he shall not share in the making and directing of the government under which he lives, than to say that he shall not acquire property and education. The fundamental and unanswerable argument in favor of the enfranchisement of the negro is found in the undisputed fact of his manhood. He is a man, and by every fact and argument by which any man can sustain his right to vote, the negro can sustain his right equally. It is plain that, if the right belongs to any, it belongs to all. The doctrine that some men have no rights that others are bound to respect, is a doctrine which we must banish, as we have banished slavery, from which it emanated. If black men have no rights in the eyes of white men, of course the whites can have none in the eyes of the blacks. The result is a war of races, and the annihilation of all proper human relations. . . .

What, then, is the work before Congress? It is to save the people of the South from themselves, and the nation from detriment on their account. Congress must supplant the evident sectional tendencies of the South by national dispositions and tendencies. It must cause national ideas and objects to take the lead and control the politics of those States. It must cease to recognize the old slavemasters as the only competent persons to rule the South. In a word, it must enfranchise the negro, and by means of the loyal negroes and the loyal white men of the South build up a national party there, and in time bridge the chasm between North and South, so that our country may have a common liberty and a common civilization.

Herbert Aptheker, "Frederick Douglass Calls for Black Suffrage in 1866," *Black Scholar*, December 1973.

DOCUMENT 11: A COMPOSITE AMERICAN NATIONALITY

In 1869, Douglass observed the growing numbers of immigrants entering the United States from Europe and Asia. Noting a wave of nativism in response to this trend, Douglass called for welcoming these new arrivals into what he hoped some day would become a "composite American nationality."

I want a home here not only for the negro, the mulatto and the Latin races, but I want the Asiatic to find a home here in the United States, and feel at home here, both for his sake and for ours. Right wrongs no man. If respect is had to majorities, the fact that only one-fifth of the population of the globe is white and the other four-fifths are colored, ought to have some weight and influence in disposing of this and similar questions. It would be a sad reflection upon the laws of nature and upon the idea of justice, to say nothing of a common Creator, if four-fifths of mankind were deprived of the rights of migration to make room for the one-fifth. If the white race may exclude all other races from this continent, it may rightfully do the same in respect to all other lands, islands, capes and continents, and thus have all the world to itself, and thus what would seem to belong to the whole would become the property of only a part. So much for what is right, now let us see what is wise.

And here I hold that a liberal and brotherly welcome to all who are likely to come to the United States is the only wise policy which this nation can adopt.

It has been thoughtfully observed that every nation, owing to its peculiar character and composition, has a definite mission in the world. What that mission is, and what policy is best adapted to assist in its fulfillment, is the business of its people and its statesmen to know, and knowing, to make a noble use of this knowledge.

I need not stop here to name or describe the missions of other and more ancient nationalities. Ours seems plain and unmistakable. Our geographical position, our relation to the outside world, our fundamental principles of government, world-embracing in their scope and character, our vast resources, requiring all manner of labor to develop them, and our already existing composite population, all conspire to one grand end, and that is, to make us the perfect national illustration of the unity and dignity of the human family that the world has ever seen.

Frederick Douglass, editorial, *Boston Daily Advertiser*, December 8, 1869.

DOCUMENT 12: THE MEANING OF THE CIVIL WAR

In the years following the Civil War, sentiment increased in the North for reconciliation with the former Confederates. Such feeling disturbed former abolitionists like Douglass who still revered the high moral purpose that the war had achieved in ending slavery. In a Memorial Day address at Arlington National Cemetery in 1871,

Douglass warned against forgetting that the North had battled for
liberty and justice while South had fought for slavery.

We are sometimes asked in the name of patriotism to forget the
merits of this fearful struggle, and to remember with equal admiration those who struck at the nation's life, and those who struck to
save it—those who fought for slavery and those who fought for liberty and justice.

I am no minister of malice. I would not strike the fallen. I would
not repel the repentant, but may my right hand forget its cunning, and
my tongue cleave to the roof of my mouth, if I forget the difference between the parties to that terrible, protracted and bloody conflict.

If we ought to forget a war which has filled our land with wid-
ows and orphans, which has made stumps of men of the very
flower of our youth, sent them on the journey of life armless, leg-
less, maimed and mutilated; which has piled up a debt heavier
than a mountain of gold—swept uncounted thousands of men into
bloody graves—and planted agony at a million hearthstones; I say
if this war is to be forgotten, I ask in the name of all things sacred
what shall men remember?

Frederick Douglass, *Life and Times of Frederick Douglass.* Hartford, CT: Park Publishing, 1881.

DOCUMENT 15: THE LEGACY OF ABRAHAM LINCOLN

Although Frederick Douglass often voiced gratitude to Abraham
Lincoln for adopting emancipation as the Union's goal in the Civil
War, he never forgot that the president had adopted that position
hesitantly. These ambivalent feelings were still strongly present in
Douglass's mind when he addressed a mass public gathering, in-
cluding President Ulysses S. Grant and other high national officials,
at the unveiling of the Freedmen's Monument to Abraham Lincoln
in Washington, D.C., in 1876.

We fully comprehend the relation of Abraham Lincoln, both to ourselves and the white people of the United States. Truth is proper and
beautiful at all times and in all places, and it is never more proper
and beautiful in any case than when speaking of a great public man
whose example is likely to be commended for honor and imitation
long after his departure to the solemn shades, the silent continents
of eternity. It must be admitted, truth compels me to admit even here
in the presence of the monument we have erected to his memory,
Abraham Lincoln was not, in the fullest sense of the word, either
our man or our model. In his interests, in his associations, in his
habits of thought, and in his prejudices, he was a white man. He
was preeminently the white man's President, entirely devoted to the
welfare of white men. He was ready and willing at any time during
the last years of his administration to deny, postpone and sacrifice
the rights of humanity in the colored people, to promote the welfare

of the white people of his country. In all his education and feelings he was an American of the Americans.

He came into the Presidential chair upon one principle alone, namely, opposition to the extension of slavery. His arguments in furtherance of this policy had their motive and mainspring in his patriotic devotion to the interest of his own race. To protect, defend and perpetuate slavery in the States where it existed, Abraham Lincoln was not less ready than any other President to draw the sword of the nation. He was ready to execute all the supposed constitutional guarantees of the Constitution in favor of the slave system anywhere inside the Slave States. He was willing to pursue, recapture, and send back the fugitive slave to his master, and to suppress a slave rising for liberty, though his guilty masters were already in arms against the Government. The race to which we belong were not the special objects of his consideration. Knowing this, I concede to you, my white fellow-citizens, a pre-eminence in this worship at once full and supreme. . . .

But while in the abundance of your wealth and in the fullness of your just and patriotic devotion you do all this, we entreat you to despise not the humble offering we this day unveil to view: for while Abraham Lincoln saved for you a country, he delivered us from a bondage, according to Jefferson, one hour of which was worse than ages of the oppression your fathers rose in rebellion to oppose.

Frederick Douglass, *Oration by Frederick Douglass Delivered on the Occasion of the Unveiling of the Freedmen's Monument in Memory of Abraham Lincoln, in Lincoln Park Washington, D.C., April 14th, 1876.* Washington, D.C.: Gibson Brothers, 1876.

DOCUMENT 14: LIBERATION OF WOMEN

Douglass and woman suffrage leaders quarreled bitterly over ratification in 1870 of the Fifteenth Amendment, enfranchising black males rather than all adults, female as well as male. Many harsh words were exchanged about the relative priority of the two reforms. By the next decade, this rift had begun to heal and Douglass was a welcomed guest at women's rights conventions such as the one in Boston in 1888 where he gave the following remarks.

My special mission in the world, if I ever had any, was the emancipation and enfranchisement of the negro. Your mission is the emancipation and enfranchisement of woman. Mine was a great cause. Yours is a much greater cause, since it comprehends the liberation and elevation of one-half of the whole human family. . . .

It is hardly necessary for me to say, after what I have already said, that I am a radical woman suffrage man. I was such a man nearly fifty years ago. I had hardly brushed the dust of slavery from my feet and stepped upon the free soil of Massachusetts, when I took the suffrage side of this question. Time, thought and experience have only increased the strength of my conviction. I believe equally in its justice, in its wisdom, and in its necessity.

But, as I understand the matter, woman does not ask man for the right of suffrage. That is something which man has no power to give. Rights do not have their source in the will or the grace of man. They are not such things as he can grant or withhold according to his sovereign will and pleasure. All that woman can properly ask man to do in this case, and all that man can do, is to get out of the way, to take his obstructive forces of fines and imprisonment and his obstructive usages out of the way, and let woman express her sentiments at the polls and in the government, equally with himself. Give her fair play and let her alone.

Philip S. Foner, ed., *Frederick Douglass on Women's Rights.* Westport, CT: Greenwood Press, 1976.

DOCUMENT 15: A PLEA FOR FAIR PLAY

In the years during and after Reconstruction, Douglass often addressed black audiences about the virtues of education and hard work. On numerous occasions, he delivered versions of a lecture entitled, "Self-Made Men." In one of his final deliveries of this lecture at the Indian Industrial School at Carlisle, Pennsylvania, in 1893, Douglass asked that the nation give African Americans a honest chance to improve themselves.

I have said "Give the negro fair play and let him alone." I meant all that I said and a good deal more than some understand by fair play. It is not fair play to start the negro out in life, from nothing and with nothing, while others start with the advantage of a thousand years behind them. He should be measured, not by the heights others have obtained, but from the depths from which he has come. For any adjustment of the scale of comparison, fair play demands that to the barbarism from which the negro started shall be added two hundred years heavy with human bondage. Should the American people put a school house in every valley of the South and a church on every hill side and supply the one with teachers and the other with preachers, for a hundred years to come, they would not then have given fair play to the negro.

The nearest approach to justice to the negro for the past is to do him justice in the present. Throw open to him the doors of the schools, the factories, the workshops, and of all mechanical industries. For his own welfare, give him a chance to do whatever he can do well. If he fails then, let him fail! I can, however, assure you that he will not fail. Already has he proven it. As a soldier he proved it. He has since proved it by industry and sobriety and by the acquisition of knowledge and property. He is almost the only successful tiller of the soil of the South, and is fast becoming the owner of land formerly owned by his old master and by the old master class. In a thousand instances has he verified my theory of self-made men. He well performed the task of making bricks without straw; now give him straw. Give him all the facilities for honest and successful livelihood, and in all honorable avocations receive him as a man among men.

Frederick Douglass, *Self-Made Men: Address Before the Students of the Indian Industrial School, Carlisle, Pa.* Carlisle, PA: Indian Print, 1893.

DOCUMENT 16: LESSONS OF THE HOUR

In his last major public lecture delivered numerous times in the early 1890s, Douglass analyzed the rising wave of antiblack violence that was sweeping the South in response to the unfairly named "Negro Problem." Douglass argued that such attacks were unprovoked and primarily intended to intimidate politically or economically assertive blacks. To Douglass, the "problem" lay not with African Americans but with the federal and state governments that failed to take civil rights abuses seriously.

But how can this [Negro] problem be solved? I will tell you how it can *not* be solved. It cannot be solved by keeping the negro poor, degraded, ignorant, and half-starved, as I have shown is now being done in the Southern States.

It cannot be solved by keeping the wages of the laborer back by fraud, as is now being done by the landlords of the South.

It cannot be done by ballot-box stuffing, by falsifying election returns, or by confusing the negro voter by cunning devices.

It cannot be done by repealing all federal laws enacted to secure honest elections.

It can, however, be done, and very easily done, for where there's a will, there's a way!

Let the white people of the North and South conquer their prejudices.

Let the great Northern press and pulpit proclaim the gospel of truth and justice against war now being made upon the negro.

Let the American people cultivate kindness and humanity.

Let the South abandon the system of "mortgage" labor, and cease to make the negro a pauper, by paying him scrip for his labor.

Let them give up the idea that they can be free, while making the negro a slave. Let them give up the idea that to degrade the colored man, is to elevate the white man.

Let them cease putting new wine into old bottles, and mending old garments with new cloth.

They are not required to do much. They are only required to undo the evil that they have done, in order to solve this problem.

In old times when it was asked, "How can we abolish slavery?" the answer was "Quit stealing."

The same is the solution of the Race problem to-day. The whole thing can be done by simply no longer violating the amendments of the Constitution of the United States, and no longer evading the claims of justice. If this were done, there would be no negro problem to vex the South, or to vex the nation.

Let the organic law of the land be honestly sustained and obeyed.

Let the political parties cease to palter in a double sense and live up to the noble declarations we find in their platforms.

Let the statesmen of the country live up to their convictions.

In the language of Senator Ingalls: "Let the nation try justice and the problem will be solved."

Frederick Douglass, *Address by Hon. Frederick Douglass, Delivered in the Metropolitan A.M.E. Church, Washington, D.C., Tuesday, January 9th, 1894, on The Lessons of the Hour.* Baltimore, MD: Thomas & Evans, 1894.

DISCUSSION QUESTIONS

CHAPTER 1

1. How did Dickson J. Preston use plantation records to trace the identity of Douglass's ancestors? Why does Preston conclude that Douglass's extended family was stable and proud? Assess the evidence for Douglass's Native American heritage.

2. Was Douglass the beneficiary of any special treatment while a young slave? How did Douglass's intelligence and ability to read affect his contentment as a slave? Assess Benjamin Quarles's claim that Douglass's master's loose control over Douglass in Baltimore only whetted the young slave's taste for complete freedom.

3. How were living conditions different for city slaves than for plantation slaves? Why did his master's negative reaction persuade Douglass of the value of literacy? Do you agree with author Gregory P. Lampe's contention that the "importance of the *Columbia Orator* in shaping Douglass'[s] future cannot be overestimated"?

CHAPTER 2

1. Tyrone Tillery argues that the split between Frederick Douglass and William Lloyd Garrison in abolitionist ranks was inevitable. Weigh the impact of such factors as personality differences, ideological disputes, and white paternalism in causing that breakup. Do you think this split would have occurred if Douglass had not spent nearly two years overseas in Great Britain?

2. Why does Leslie Friedman Goldstein conclude that Douglass selected the tactics of a reformer to advance his radical abolitionist goals? How did differing schools of abolitionists view the relationship of slavery to the U.S. Constitution? What tactics did Douglass employ to encourage the political system to advance his abolitionist objectives?

3. What arguments of John Brown did Douglass incorporate into his own condemnation of slavery? How did Brown attempt to recruit Douglass into his violent plot, and why did he fail? Do you agree with author James H. Cook's harsh appraisal of Douglass's refusal to follow Brown?

4. Why does historian Christopher N. Breiseth conclude that by 1865 Douglass and Abraham Lincoln shared a similar vision of the causes and consequences of the Civil War? Why was Douglass disappointed with Lincoln's policies early in the war? How did the debate over blacks in military service bring the two men together?

CHAPTER 3

1. David W. Blight contends that Frederick Douglass believed that African Americans had a special interest in preserving the memory of the Civil War. What was the myth of the Lost Cause, and why did Douglass argue against it? Do you believe that Douglass succeeded in shaping the legacy of the importance of the Civil War?

2. Why does Waldo E. Martin Jr. conclude that Douglass struggled "ingeniously, yet unsuccessfully, to resolve his ambivalence" on issues of race? How did Douglass believe that the nation's race problems could be resolved through assimilation into a "composite American nationality"?

3. Do you believe that historian Merline Pitre has proven that Douglass sympathized with American "imperialist aspirations" against Haiti? In what ways did racial attitudes affect the American-Haitian negotiations? If Douglass supported American imperialism, how do you account for the Haitians' hiring of Douglass to represent them at the World's Columbian Exposition in Chicago?

4. Speculate on why the racial attitudes of Europeans toward Douglass were different than those he encountered in the United States. Why did Douglass react so negatively toward the Roman Catholic Church? Why does author Philip S. Foner conclude that as a black man Douglass had noticed "things which were ignored by most travelers"?

CHAPTER 4

1. What qualities did both Booker T. Washington and W.E.B. Du Bois believe that Frederick Douglass exemplified? Why does Washington regard Douglass as representing the common experiences of nineteenth-century African Americans? Why does Du Bois contend that Douglass preferred to argue from the basis of humanity rather than race?

2. Wilson J. Moses complains that Douglass has been allowed

to largely dictate the terms of his own historical image. Is Moses correct that Douglass was not representative of the black experience of his era? Why does Moses conclude that Douglass was unfair in acknowledging the accomplishments of most of his black contemporaries? Is it correct to characterize Douglass as a total assimilationist?

CHRONOLOGY

1818

Frederick Augustus Washington Bailey is born sometime in February at Holme Hill Farm, Talbot County, Maryland.

1826

Douglass is sent to live with Hugh Auld's family in Baltimore.

1833

Douglass is retuned to his master, Thomas Auld, at St. Michaels, Maryland.

1834

Douglass spends a year as a field hand hired out to Talbot County "slave breaker" Edward Covey.

1836

After Douglass unsuccessfully attempts to escape, he is sent back to the household of Thomas Auld in Baltimore.

1838

On September 3 Douglass escapes slavery and flees to the North. He marries Anna Murray in New York City on September 15, and the couple settles in New Bedford, Massachusetts.

1841

After addressing an antislavery meeting in Nantucket, Massachusetts, Douglass is hired as a lecturer by colleagues of abolitionist publisher William Lloyd Garrison.

1845

Douglass publishes his first autobiography, *Narrative of the Life of Frederick Douglass, an American Slave,* making his identity public and thus placing himself in danger of being recaptured as a runaway slave. For his safety, Douglass departs in August for Great Britain on an abolitionist lecture tour.

1847

Douglass returns to the United States in April. From a new home in Rochester, New York, Douglass publishes the first issue of his weekly newspaper, the *North Star*, on December 3.

1848

Douglass attends the Seneca Falls Women's Rights Convention between July 19 and 20.

1851

After breaking from the Garrisonian abolitionists, Douglass revamps his newspaper into *Frederick Douglass' Paper*, a Liberty Party vehicle.

1852

On July 5 Douglass delivers his most memorable oration, "What to the Slave Is the Fourth of July?," in Rochester, New York.

1853

Douglass publishes a novella, "The Heroic Slave," a fictionalized account of a real slave uprising.

1855

Douglass's second autobiography, *My Bondage and My Freedom*, is published.

1858

Douglass starts publishing *Douglass's Monthly* in Rochester.

1859

Following the doomed Harpers Ferry raid in October, Douglass flees first to Canada and then to Great Britain for safety when evidence is uncovered of his close connections with the raid's leader, John Brown. He remains abroad until April 1860.

1863

After recruiting black troops for the Union army, Douglass has the first of three private interviews with President Abraham Lincoln. Douglass encourages Lincoln to allow black soldiers to demonstrate their capabilities in combat against the Confederate army.

1870

Douglass relocates to Washington, D.C., and begins editing the weekly *New National Era* to advance black civil rights as well as other reforms.

1871

In the position of secretary, Douglass accompanies a special U.S. commission sent to investigate possibilities for annexation of the Dominican Republic.

1874

Appointed president of the Freedman's Savings Bank in March, Douglass has to close the institution due to insolvency in July.

1877

President Rutherford B. Hayes appoints Douglass U.S. marshal of the District of Columbia.

1879

Douglass publicly opposes the black exodus from the South to Kansas and other prairie states.

1881

President James A. Garfield appoints Douglass recorder of the deeds for the District of Columbia.

1882

In January Douglass publishes the first edition of his last autobiography, *Life and Times of Frederick Douglass.* In August, Douglass's wife, Anna, dies.

1884

Douglass's marriage in January to a younger white woman, Helen Pitts, causes a public controversy.

1886

In September Douglass and his new wife depart for a tour of Europe and the Near East, returning in August 1887.

1887

Douglass accepts the appointment as U.S. ambassador to Haiti in July.

1889

Douglass resigns his diplomatic post in August after clashes with the administration of Benjamin Harrison over attempted annexation of a Haitian port to serve as an American naval base.

1892

In October Douglass begins serving as the commissioner of Haitian pavilion at the World's Columbian Exposition in

Chicago. He holds that position until December 1893 and meets many of the next generation of African American leaders.

1895

Douglass dies at his Cedar Hill home in Washington, D.C., on February 20 after attending a women's rights convention.

FOR FURTHER RESEARCH

AUTOBIOGRAPHIES

Life and Times of Frederick Douglass. Hartford, CT: Park Brothers, 1881.

My Bondage and My Freedom. New York: Miller, Orton, & Mulligan, 1855.

Narrative of the Life of Frederick Douglass, an American Slave. Boston: Anti-Slavery Office, 1845.

COLLECTIONS OF ORIGINAL DOCUMENTS BY FREDERICK DOUGLASS

John W. Blassingame et al., eds., *The Frederick Douglass Papers.* Series 1. *Speeches, Debates, and Interviews.* 5 vols. New Haven, CT: Yale University Press, 1979–1992.

Philip S. Foner, ed., *Frederick Douglass on Women's Rights.* Westport, CT: Greenwood, 1976.

——, *The Life and Writings of Frederick Douglass.* 5 vols. New York: International, 1950–1975.

Michael McCurdy, ed., *Escape from Slavery: The Boyhood of Frederick Douglass in His Own Words.* New York: Alfred A. Knopf, 1994.

Milton Meltzer, ed., *Frederick Douglass, in His Own Words.* San Diego: Harcourt Brace, 1995.

BIOGRAPHIES AND STUDIES OF FREDERICK DOUGLASS

William Andrews, ed., *The Oxford Frederick Douglass Reader.* New York: Oxford University Press, 1996.

Evelyn Bennett, *Frederick Douglass and the War Against Slavery.* Brookfield, CT: Millbrook, 1993.

David W. Blight, *Frederick Douglass' Civil War: Keeping the*

Faith in Jubilee. Baton Rouge: Louisiana State University Press, 1989.

Maria Dietrich, *Love Across Color Lines: Ottilie Assing and Frederick Douglass.* New York: Hill and Wang, 1999.

Philip S. Foner, *Frederick Douglass.* New York: Citadel, 1950.

James M. Gregory, *Frederick Douglass, the Orator.* 1893. Reprint, New York: Apollo Editions, 1971.

Nathan Irvin Huggins, *Slave and Citizen: The Life of Frederick Douglass.* Ed. Oscar Handlin. Boston: Little, Brown, 1980.

Sheila Keenan, *Frederick Douglass: Portrait of a Freedom Fighter.* New York: Scholastic, 1995.

Waldo E. Martin Jr., *The Mind of Frederick Douglass.* Chapel Hill: University of North Carolina Press, 1984.

William S. McFeely, *Frederick Douglass.* New York: W.W. Norton, 1991.

Patricia McKissack and Fredrick McKissack, *Frederick Douglass: The Black Lion.* Chicago: Children's Press, 1987.

Douglass T. Miller, *Frederick Douglass and the Fight for Freedom.* New York: Facts On File, 1988.

Dickson J. Preston, *Young Frederick Douglass: The Maryland Years.* Baltimore: Johns Hopkins University Press, 1980.

Benjamin Quarles, *Frederick Douglass.* New York: Atheneum, 1968.

Sharman Apt Russell, *Frederick Douglass.* New York: Chelsea House, 1988.

Frederick S. Voss, *Majestic in His Wrath: A Pictorial Life of Frederick Douglass.* Washington, DC: Smithsonian Institution, 1995.

Booker T. Washington, *Frederick Douglass.* Philadelphia: George W. Jacobs, 1906.

GENERAL HISTORIES OF THE ABOLITIONIST AND EARLY CIVIL RIGHTS MOVEMENTS

Herbert Aptheker, *Abolitionism: A Revolutionary Movement.* Boston: Twayne, 1989.

Merton L. Dillon, *Slavery Attacked: Southern Slaves and*

Their Allies, 1619–1865. Baton Rouge: Louisiana State University Press, 1990.

Barbara Jeanne Fields, *Slavery and Freedom on the Middle Ground: Maryland in the Nineteenth Century.* New Haven, CT: Yale University Press, 1985.

Lawrence J. Friedman, *Gregarious Saints: Self and Community in American Abolitionism, 1830–1870.* New York: Cambridge University Press, 1983.

Lawrence Levine, *Black Culture and Black Consciousness: Afro-American Folk Thought from Slavery to Freedom.* New York: Oxford University Press, 1977.

James M. McPherson, *The Abolitionist Legacy: From Reconstruction to the NAACP.* Princeton, NJ: Princeton University Press, 1975.

Wilson J. Moses, *The Golden Age of Black Nationalism, 1850–1925.* Hamden, CT: Archon Books, 1978.

Nell Irvin Painter, *Exodusters: Black Migration to Kansas After Reconstruction.* New York: Knopf, 1976.

Jane H. Pease and William H. Pease, *They Who Would Be Free: Blacks' Search for Freedom, 1830–1861.* New York: Atheneum, 1974.

John Stauffer, *The Black Hearts of Men: Radical Abolitionists and the Transformation of Race.* Cambridge, MA: Harvard University Press, 2002.

James Brewer Stewart, *Holy Warriors: The Abolitionists and American Slavery.* 2nd ed. New York: Hill and Wang, 1997.

Joel Williamson, *The Crucible of Race: Black/White Relations in the American South Since Emancipation.* New York: Oxford University Press, 1984.

C. Vann Woodward, *The Strange Career of Jim Crow.* 3rd rev. ed. New York: Oxford University Press, 1974.

INDEX